The Mystery of Suffering

Freedom From
or
Presence Within
Suffering

James Lindemann

PROOF COPY

RFLindemann & Son, Publisher

2013

James (Jim) Lindemann

Webpage: lindespirit.com
email: jim@lindespirit.com
Blog: CovenantMusings.lindespirit.com

Other titles by the author:
COVENANT: The Blood Is The Life
Creation's Ballet for Jesus
Celebration! - Holy Communion: A Love Story
In the Image of God: Male and Female He Created Them
Living Waters: Baptism – From His Heart Through Ours

RFL & Son, Publisher
541 33 Street South
Lethbridge, Alberta, Canada T1J 3V7

ISBN 978-0-9916866-9-8

Flyleaf

Dr Paul Brand had thought that pain was God's one great mistake, but in working with lepers in India and in North America who because of disease lack this sensation, he realized that pain is essential in keeping us alive: it is the warning system that something is wrong, even lethally wrong. It is no surprise then after Adam and Eve's fall into sin, that God "turns up the pain," the suffering which warns that there is something deadly in our world and in our lives which really requires attention.

But not to be merely dismissed as punishment for sin, in the hands of Him Who loves us, God's design is that such affliction ultimately challenges faith and brings out hidden and often unrealized strengths. Even in the extreme crucible of Nazi and Japanese World War II death camps, with death and suffering overwhelmingly everywhere, where the nominal faith focused on ease and prosperity is abandoned, a faith with real substance is discovered.

It is a faith with concrete comfort particularly because of the presence of Jesus Who intimately knows pain and intimately knows us. As Job was never told why he suffered, so suffering may remain a mystery for us as well, at least during the time of distress. Still, we are also given clues as to the effect which pain can have in making our faith and life far richer than would be possible without it. It provides essential threads within the tapestry which one day will be revealed as the beautiful wisdom of a God of Love and wonderful Glory.

The Author

The author, a pastor himself, is the recipient of perspectives, concerns and interests handed down from a long line of pastors in the Lutheran Church, hence his interest and background in such things as the Sacraments, the Covenant, and even the Star of Bethlehem. His Bible Study groups have also contributed greatly in developing these various themes, and now as retirement approaches, this is a good time to gather these thoughts into a more finished form.

Born and raised in New York City, he has come to also value the life in the smaller communities. With his deeply appreciated companion (his wife), their family bulges at the seams with four natural, two adopted, a variety of foster children, and now grandchildren – there is no end to the usually delightful competition for his attention. Perhaps in the coming years there may even be time to pursue his Master's interest in carpentry.

Table of Contents

Preface   vii

1. The Cold Slap in the Face   1
The Holy Innocents ... Can God Really Handle Evil? ... The Relationship of Humans to God ... The Risk of Love ... The Dilemma of Love ... The Fallen Angel ... The Buck Stops Here ... Overwhelming Suffering ... Keeping the End in Sight ... A Word About Faith ... Suffering Faith

2. Life and Pain   19
Death ... The Lord from Heaven to Earth Descends ... Pain and Death ... Pain: The Gift Nobody Wants ... "I will Greatly Increase Your Toil/Pain" ... Leprosy ... The Reality of Eternal Death ... The Lepers ... His Own Medicine

3. Submission   35
Ravensbruck ... Did Your God of Love Will This? ... Hypocrisy ... The Dark Side of Free Will ... To Be [a God] or Not To Be ... To Obey Him ... Walking in Them ... The Other Hypocrisy ... The Light of God

4. The Larger Picture   49
Blameless ... "To Destroy Him Without Cause" ... Preparing the Stage ... Worship?? ... Realistic? ... "The Dark Night of the Soul" ... Faith Within Suffering ... Equipped and Empowered ... The Redeemer

5. Expanding Ripples   73
The Bridge over San Luis Rey ... Complexity ... Job's Wife ... The Perpetrator ... The Holy Innocents ... "There is a Season, and a Time" ... Too Much to Handle ... Not Immune

6. The Breadth of Repentance   91
Repent! (The Plea and Warning to Repent ... The Suffering of the Forgiven) Hereditary and Collective Sin (Collective Sin ... Collective Responsibility ... Why Collective Responsibility? ... Generational Sin) Have a Good Day

7. Innumerable Tasks   105
Unique Wisdom ... Pruned ... Refining ... Taking up the Cross Daily ... "Righteous" vs "Good"–Doing What is Right ... "Necessary" Evil ... When You Hate Your Job-Jeremiah Again

8. More of the Mosaic   127
Sources (Satan ... The World ... "The Fifth Column" ... Nature) Choosing to Suffer (Selfishness and Altruism ... Understanding Altruism ... When Love Runs Toward Suffering ... God's Chosen Suffering to End Suffering ... Just Plain Grit)

9. The Last Chapter, Not the Last Word **145**

A Continuing Story … Confidence … Love … Father! … Confidence (Reprise) … Contentment … "That We May Comfort" … Prayer … Suffering's Ultimate Conclusion … Joy

Endnotes **165**

Preface

In the time before television – yes, there was such a time –, a radio situation comedy was called "Fibber McGee and Molly," in which there was a notorious closet. Invariably a guest or friend would innocently go to open the closet door and the warning would ring out, "Don't open that door!!!" Alas, the warning would come too late and there would be for what seemed to be a full minute's worth of the clatter of items falling out of the closet.

Suffering can seem like that closet. It is such a topic that once the door is opened there seems to be no end as to what is stored inside. That is the first intimidation about writing on this subject: there is no way to have the last word; there is always something more, some other Bible passage, some other experience, some other perspective which could and should be included. CS Lewis wrote a little book entitled, *The Problem of Pain*, in which he did a remarkable job in discussing the logic and theory of the Christian viewpoint on pain. There is indeed comfort in having a roadmap of sorts when encountering the territory of pain and suffering, to know the heading and the landscape where such things may take us. Yet this knowledge does not insulate against the realities. In a most pronounced way, theory would meet experience years later when his wife of three years died of cancer. Even though he had married her fully aware of what she was battling, his account, *A Grief Observed*, describes the reality in counterpoint to his theory – not as a denial but as an enhancement to his thoughts.

Still, as his step-son observes in his preface to *A Grief Observed*, the indefinite "A" in the title is essential. Lewis' experience is not necessarily a model of all grief nor of all suffering. The variations are just too many and too wide. In writing about suffering, there will always be the question, "but what about …?" – and one more item falls out of the closet.

This book is the result of a three-plus hour and other discussions with two friends and is the attempt to investigate some of the questions on which we jointly wrestled. Yet there is still a deep sense of inadequacy, wondering if the answers could not be better, knowing that not all the questions have been answered, and knowing that not all the questions *can* be answered.

The second intimidation is as Lewis wrote in *The Problem of Pain's* chapter VI:

> All arguments in justification of suffering provoke bitter resentment against the author. You would like to know how I behave when I am experiencing pain, not writing books about it. You need not guess, for I will tell you; I am a great coward. But what is that to the purpose? When I think of pain ... it "quite o'ercrows my spirit". If I knew any way of escape I would crawl through sewers to find it. But what is the good of telling you about my feelings? You know them already: they are the same as yours. I am not arguing that pain is not painful. Pain hurts. That is what the word means. I am only trying to show that the old Christian doctrine of being made "perfect through suffering" is not incredible. To prove it palatable is beyond my design.
>
> CS Lewis[1]

I also am a coward when it comes to pain. As I look at those who have contributed to this subject both in the Bible and outside of it, not in the sterile atmosphere of an essay but in the crucible of suffering in their lives, I am grateful for two things: one, that I have not had to experience some of these depths myself. This does not mean that I am untested, only that in God's mercy I have not had to endure the degree and extent of their situations – although as Lewis experienced, that may also come for me. But what is useful is that those who have shared their extreme experience have provided a concrete foundation beyond what some may discard as merely theoretical imaginings.

Unfortunately the tendency is indeed to treat the subject in a philosophical tone, rather than in the personal struggle of actual human beings. We are surprisingly quick to become desensitized in many ways: a case in point is the Cross of Jesus where we have developed the seeming attitude that although he did have "some discomfort," it meant little because He knew He would rise on the third day; or that the Father casually watched His beloved Son die, because He would soon be risen from the dead anyway. Perhaps that is oversimplifying our reactions, but we do seem to quickly develop a callous in regard to others, even to God, in their suffering.

The other danger, of course, is to so overaccent the sentimentality that the discussion descends into a maudlin burlesque of the power of suffering.

Yet there are also times when something connects to our own experience of pain, which then restores the subject to the true-to-life struggle of which we are all too familiar. It is to realize what Tom Long concluded in his article on "Preaching About Suffering":

> The Christian "answer" to the problem of suffering and evil, then, is not a philosophical claim that allows one to say, "Now this explains it, this solves the problem," but rather a retelling of the Christian story in such a way that people are enabled to live one more day, one more hour with the anguish. Tom Long[2]

That is the hope behind the discussion in this book.

Jim Lindemann

September, 2013

Postscript:

Likely with varying degrees of accuracy, the Bible quote translations are mine, however there is a heavy dependence on:

The Interlinear Hebrew/Greek English Bible, 4 volumes
    Jay Green, ed., (Lafayette, IN: Associated Publishers and Authors, 1979)

As well as
The Online Bible computer program (http://www.onlinebible.net)
        Copyright in Canada
        by Larry Pierce
            (11 Holmwood St., Winterbourne, Ontario, N0B 2V0)

and particularly its modules for

   The Authorized or King James (1769) Version

American King James Version
    Michael Peter (Stone) Engelbrite (True Grace Ministries)
    Placed into the public domain on November 8, 1999.

also its dictionary linking to *Strong's Concordance* numbers and to

   R Laird Harris, *Theological Wordbook of the Old Testament* (Chicago: Moody Press, 1981)

   Gerhard Kittel and Gerhard Friedrich, ed., *Theological Dictionary of the New Testament*, (Grand Rapids, MI: Wm. B. Eerdmans Publishing Co., 1966).

1. The Cold Slap in the Face

The Holy Innocents

With all the Good News, joy and peace accented during Christmas, it is a bit of a jolt that immediately following this holiday comes a day set aside to remember "The Holy Innocents." The occasion is that when the Magi come seeking the One "Who is born King of the Jews" [Matthew 2:2], King Herod tells them to return to him when they find this King so that he might also "worship" Him (actually to kill Him).

However, Jehovah commands the Magi to *not* return to Herod, which naturally enrages the king. Already the agenda both of Satan and of mankind to be rid of God at any cost is revealed as Herod orders the death of boys two years and under around Bethlehem in order to remove this threat [Matthew 2:16-18], and therefore

> A voice in Ramah was heard, weeping and great mourning, Rachel weeping for her children and would not be comforted because they are no more.   Matthew 2:18

The death of any child often evokes strong emotional response, but deliberate murder is like pulling the rug out from under the spirit of Christmas. So as the Magi leave and are warned to return by a different way (in order to avoid Herod); and as Joseph is warned by an angel to immediately take his family and flee to Egypt, what they leave behind are legitimate questions: where does suffering come from? why do the innocent suffer? And where is God in all of this?

1

Can God Really Handle Evil?

Recently there was the annual memorial to the over two thousand innocent men, women and children who died when the two World Trade Towers in New York were attacked and fell on September 11, 2001. It is evident that the same questions have echoed throughout the generations not just from "the Holy Innocents," but as far back as Job and even earlier, until today. Some simply dismiss the possibility of a good, if any, God, while others try to make what would seem a reasonable compromise with what they have observed.

Rabbi Harold Kushner, in his book *When Bad Things Happen to Good People*, is one of many who repeat in one form or another the argument of the Greek philosopher Epicurus (341 - 270 BC) who stated that if an all-powerful and perfectly good God exists, then evil cannot exist (how can a good God allow it, and why would He not in His omniscience and power prevent it?). But since there is evil in the world, then such a God does not exist.

Although Kushner tries to protect the idea that God exists, still he uses this "straw man" (something that is deliberately constructed in order to "knock it down," to force certain conclusions) argument as he attempts to integrate his experience with his worldview. He wants to keep God as good and loving, just and fair; Someone with Whom to talk and share the journey of our lives; but since there is evil in this world, he concludes that God must also be helpless against and caught off guard by its intrusion.

Such a God as simply a nice Person ultimately means that there is nothing that He can bring to the table of suffering beyond what any mere human can bring: a listening ear and a willingness to walk with us. Yet is there really nothing more that the Creator of the Universe has to offer?

If indeed the Creator is good and loving, just and fair, there is need to identify the source of the evil which intrudes into His creation. Is it some equivalent to God, and perhaps His superior, since He can seem powerless to anticipate, much less to thwart it? And if this is so now, then evil will invade *any* creation of God forever – there will be no relief, no answer to it. There will be no heaven, just a continuation of what we have now. Unless this question is addressed, rather than "protecting" the concept of God, the rabbi basically condemns us to a God Who is inept to help, despite how He might be a pretty nice guy.

> Either the day must come when joy prevails and all the makers of misery are no longer able to infect it, or else, for ever and ever, the makers of misery can destroy in others the happiness they reject for themselves.
>
> CS Lewis[3]

The Relationship of Humans to God

Why do humans exist? This is no incidental question! The intended role of Creation, and particularly of humanity, has a great deal of bearing on the reality of evil. In the book *In the Image of God: Male and Female He Created Them*, the present author begins:

> It is obvious that God is hidden from our view.
> But do you realize that this is *on purpose*?
> He has no physical form by which we can recognize Him or see Him at work. Yet this is no accident – He planned it this way. He could have created an environment where He would be continually "in plain sight" – after all, on the Last Day, in "the new heaven and the new earth," there will be no trouble seeing Him in all His majesty.
> Yet His choice has been a visible universe in which *He* would be invisible – why? why has He created it this way? And how then are we – indeed all Creation – to catch any glimpses of Him? ...
> ... Yes, we can see His power and deity, but where might His creatures find His heart? ...
> God said, "Let Us make man in Our Image, according to Our Likeness: and let them rule..."   Genesis 1:26

There is a way by which He can be "seen", although not directly. He designs a *mirror*, something that would reflect Him, something that would bear His "Image," something that would represent Him ("rule") before all Creation. He fashions a man from the dust of the ground and places into his nostrils His own Breath [Genesis 2:7].

Here is one of the great mysteries about the great Jehovah, something we would never have imagined. On one hand, He is supremely self-sufficient – He obviously needs no one to accomplish His will: He does not *need* angels and, for that matter, He really doesn't need *us* either. In fact, one might think that we humans too often get in His way and are too much of a bother and a liability for what He wants to do.

Yet His *design* is to make *us* be *an essential partner* in what He does. He chooses to have humans be His physical representatives before Creation. Here is to be demonstrated those characteristics of the Creator that cannot be found in the stars and the planets, nor in the mountains and the seas, nor in the plants and animals. Here is to be the Image of God's *heart*.   James Lindemann[4]

The last two paragraphs in the quote are most significant. We seem to have the idea that, for example, humanity was created to "occupy space" in God's creation, that the Creator merely wanted something that would basically love and worship Him. Yet God is looking for *partners*, where things will not happen in this Creation unless done by only *human* hands:, such as, feeding the hungry, clothing the naked, taking care of the earth, even having the Good News of Jesus brought to others. He really, really means it – however, if a parent gives his child a responsibility, the child must be able to make his own decisions, of which there are always consequences, which most often affects others in some way. Just as the parent cannot keep "rescuing" the situation by jumping in to do the chores which the child must do, neither God nor the angels will fill the gap when humans are negligent.

God does not brush aside this high position after Adam and Eve's sin – the commission has never been withdrawn. He is that intent about the honor and responsibility He has placed upon us. This then opens a profound risk for Love.

The Risk of Love

The design is that God's heart is to be fleshed out into humanity. It is a partnership requiring mutual Love to bind it together, as humanity reflects divinity to the *cosmos* ("We Love, because He first Loved us" [I John 4:19]). To reflect Jehovah's Love, which is freely given, the human then must also have a love freely to give. His Love cannot be manipulation, by making us think that we are choosing when we really are not (a sort of "Matrix" movie scenario). A puppet can only mechanically feign, it cannot Love: it cannot receive nor express its Creator's Love as a true partner, neither back to God nor outward to Creation.

And would this really be Love on God's part or simply lifeless control? Does God really need robots?

He chose to Love, His Love is freely given, and because of that, His Love is creative – that is how we came into existence to begin with. How then are we to reflect Him, if we are not allowed to love, to choose to love or to not love? The human must therefore have the option to "not love." It certainly does highlight the dilemma into which God places Himself. It is no casual decision for Him to allow humans to choose, instead it is one which really does come from His heart. But what if this creature who holds such a key position in the universe rejects this relationship to the Creator? This alternative would allow catastrophic results, since humanity is the pivot for the mutual communication between the Maker with his Creation.

Creation – the "cosmos" – looks to "the Image of God" to see its beloved Creator's face and characteristics (Steadfast Love and the rest), in order to recover its balance, but something is wrong. Something has happened to "the Image." …

Man looks not to the heart of God but rather into his own heart. Although created in "the Image of God" [Genesis 5:1], he fathers "a son in his own 'soul-likeness,' after his own image" [v 3]. The reflecting pool is churned up by the storm of sin. Rather than the demonstration

5

of God's Glory, instead there is selfishness, greed, plunder, callousness, hatred and destruction – is it any wonder that Creation has become as chaotic as the human heart? James Lindemann[5]

Or as St Paul put it:

> For in earnest expectation, Creation expectantly awaits the revealing of the sons of God. For Creation was subjected to aimlessness and corruption, not voluntarily, but because of Him Who subjected it in hope; because the Creation also will be freed from the slavery of corruption into the freedom of the Glory of the children of God. For we know that the whole Creation groans and travails together until now.
>
> Romans 8:19-22

This provides a glimpse of the enormous privilege and significance of the human within the universe, increased by magnitudes by the fact that God would even become a human in order to save us. If He is truly serious about His intended position and honor for humanity, then such *universal* ramifications are a necessary risk.

The Dilemma of Love

What the rabbi misses is a realistic depiction of particularly God's Love, which, at least in the world which we now have, creates a tension: the Lord's giving the choice to humans itself creates suffering – *His* suffering, as when the parent is rejected by a child (consider the prodigal son parable; and Adam and Eve's fall) – if the parent didn't care, then there would be no suffering –; or when the Father watches His Son give His life in order to save "outsiders" (as when the parent watches the son go off to war to rescue those in the clutches of cruelty). Unfortunately but realistically, suffering and Love are linked.

Imagine how He suffers when He must watch people's terrible and cruel choices which create torment in the humanity He has personally handcrafted – especially when He knows all this in far more detail than we! Before

6

Christmas in 2012, twenty-six children and adults were killed in a school in a mass murder in Newtown, Connecticut. Just imagine what it must be like for Him, Who saw what would happen in Newtown, what would happen in millions and millions of other such events throughout history, knowing that this would be the result if He allows humans to choose to not love.

Did it make Him hesitate? He knew that if He went ahead and gave humanity the ability to not love, His beloved Son would end up on a Cross for creatures who would barely, if ever, stop to acknowledge Him, much less to honor Him, much less to even love Him in return. That would be the most costly result of them all. That is where it would hit the closest to home – that is where He knew He would stand alongside the grieving parents as He Himself would come to understand grief. His dilemma is that if indeed He Loves, then He must suffer; yet if indeed He Loves, then He must also allow the choices which cause His own heart to break. He knows the cost, not just for all Creation but also personally for Him.

How many times does a parent, through love, allow "evil" or even create "suffering" for the child? Although we want love to be sweetness and light and warm and fuzzy, there are times when it requires a certain grittiness and heaviness of heart. A parent may need to "bite the lip" as something is withheld, or in allowing a situation to come to its logical consequences, or may apply some other kind of discipline/punishment. Even if a parent attempts to "fix" a problem for the child, it may actually be the greater evil in the long term, so that the parent must "turn a deaf ear" either to the person with responsibility or to the victim. Just as when the fledgling is pushed out of the nest, there can be a lot more to "good and loving, just and fair" than simply what may be nice and comfortable.

So Jehovah is no mere unimpassioned by-stander, and He knows the extreme to which His suffering will go because of His Love: it will take Him to a Cross above Jerusalem, to forsakenness and death; yet what else could He do, if He Loves? Yet that very Love and suffering will bring His heartfelt outcome where even when we were

> ... dead in trespasses, He made us alive with Christ – by grace you are being saved – and "jointly raised up" and "jointly seated" us in the heavenly places in Christ Jesus, so that He might show in the coming ages the surpassing riches of His grace in kindness toward us in Christ Jesus.   Ephesians 2:4-7

The result is the heart-felt goal of being "jointly seated" with Him:

> The Word is faithful: if we "jointly died" with Him, then we shall "jointly live" with Him; if we persevere, then we shall "jointly reign" with Him ...   II Timothy 2:11-12

Joined to Christ, we will experience the fulfillment of His suffering and Love as the high honor for humanity, which is declared in the very first chapter of the Bible, is fulfilled forever.

The Fallen Angel

There is another player in this drama. Apparently there is a parallel honor and responsibility given to the angels which also focuses on Love, therefore they also are a key pivot in the running of perhaps a more encompassing Creation. Again, the Creator does not "need" help, yet He chooses to have His creatures be more than mere bystanders and cheering sections – He wants their participation in the management of His Creation(s). But then again the risk of "to not Love" raises its head, and this high value placed upon these creatures can also be rejected as well.

As Ezekiel 28:12-17 recounts, "Lucifer" had been privileged to represent God in a heavenly Garden of Eden, where the scene is in crystalline material rather than plants:

... You had the seal of the consummation of the full measure of wisdom and perfect beauty; you were in Eden – the garden of God – every precious stone was your covering: ruby, topaz, diamond, beryl, onyx, jasper, sapphire, turquoise, emerald, and gold; ... You were the anointed overseeing cherub, I placed you on the holy mountain of God [often a poetic symbol for God's rule], in the settings (stones) of fire you walked. You were blameless in your ways from the day you were created, until iniquity was found in you. In the abundance of your trade [carrying God's will, carrying creation's worship] you were filled with "violence"/greed, and you rebelled ... Your heart was lifted up because of your beauty; your wisdom corrupted because of your splendor. ...

Satan chose instead to reflect his own heart, to be in his own "image" – note the reoccurrence of the "I":

How you have fallen from the heavens, O shining one, son of the morning! You are cut down to the earth, you who prostrated the nations! You said in your heart: "I will ascend upwards, to the very stars of God I will raise my throne; I will sit on the mount of assembly at the rear of the [hall of the] north; I will ascend above the heights of the clouds**, I will be the Highest!"   Isaiah 14:12-14
        *poetic symbol of God's dwelling and rule: "assembly" – perhaps parallel to Job 1:6;2:1].
        **"clouds" is often the poetic description of the vast company of angels.

Although not the equal of the Creator, there is now a malevolent being who is marked by hatred, "a liar and a murderer from the beginning" [John 8:44]. It is hard to imagine what this hatred must be like, since there is no redeeming feature about it. It arises out of a loathing of God and everything related to Him – after all, the very existence of the Lord stands against everything which Satan wants to be and to do. Since Love is the earmark of the Creator, then whatever the Devil has has none of this. And even sinful humanity, following in his footsteps, has no real loyalty to Satan, since "All we like sheep have gone astray; each of us has turned to his own path" [Isaiah 53:6].

The Buck Stops Here

Forming light and creating darkness, making peace [shalom] and creating affliction – I am Jehovah, Who does all these things.   Isaiah 45:7

"The Buck Stops Here" is the phrase US President Harry S Truman made famous, which indicates that the president – here God – has to make the final decisions and bear their ultimate responsibility for what happens. This is visible in the book of Job and in this following account of the prophet Micaiah relating to King Ahab the scene in Heaven, where in both incidents it seems that the Lord deliberately baits the Devil, with the sad irony being that struggle as Satan will against God, anything he does is only by permission:

> A spirit came and stood before Jehovah, and said, 'I will entice him.' Jehovah said to him, 'How so?' So he said, 'I will go and become a deceiving spirit in the mouth of all his prophets.' Jehovah said, 'You shall entice him and moreover prevail; go and do so.' Now behold! Jehovah has put a deceiving spirit in the mouth of these your prophets – Jehovah has declared evil against you.
> II Chronicles 18:20-22; also I Kings 22:21-23

Satan is but a creature – God is neither weak nor ineffectual before this source of evil, but rather is fully and completely in charge. But as He demonstrates His final say in regard to all things, even tragedies, it still is difficult. Although such things do not happen "by His own hand," that they happen at all is laid at the foot of His throne. Why has He allowed for Satan, much less evil, to remain? Evidently He wishes for evil to run its full course, not for *His* benefit but rather for *the sake of the Creation(s)*. What then is the Creation(s) to discover and come to understand about evil? Possibly by seeing malevolence at work with its results laid bare, those who choose reciprocal Love will be confirmed and solidified in their decision, while the character of evil's rebellion will be revealed in its terrible desires, and in its ensuing and in its ultimate consequences.

Given that Jehovah is Love, allowing evil cannot be a casual decision on His part. There is nothing more antithetical to Himself than for what evil stands and in what it results. Therefore whatever He is revealing about this darkness in the Creation(s) must be of such utmost importance, that allowing it to have its day is absolutely necessary despite how distasteful it is to Himself and even bewildering to us.

Overwhelming Suffering

CS Lewis, in his *The Problem of Pain*, states:

> We must never make the problem of pain worse than it is by vague talk about the "unimaginable sum of human misery". Suppose that I have a toothache of intensity x: and suppose that you, who are seated beside me, also begin to have a toothache of intensity x. You may, if you choose, say that the total amount of pain in the room is now 2x. But you must remember that no one is suffering 2x: search all time and all space and you will not find that composite pain in anyone's consciousness. There is no such thing as a sum of suffering, for no one suffers it. When we have reached the maximum that a single person can suffer, we have, no doubt, reached something very horrible, but we have reached all the suffering there ever can be in the universe. The addition of a million fellow-sufferers adds no more pain.[6]

Truly we sometimes exaggerate suffering by lumping it all together, when the reality is that one can only suffer his own pain. We simply build a case for personal despair by unrealistically creating an impossible burden of suffering, by which Satan can effectively defeat us or make us *catatonic* ("catatonic": a physical condition marked by muscular rigidity and mental stupor; although here it would mean spiritually and mentally unable to move).

Except…

Surely He has borne our calamities and carried our agonies; yet we judged Him as punished, struck by God, and oppressed. But He was wounded for our rebellion, He was crushed for our iniquities; the chastisement for our peace [*shalom* – wholeness] was upon Him, and by His stripes we are healed.   Isaiah 53:4-5

Yes, there is a lump sum of suffering, and there is One Who does bear it *all*. In our discussion, we must account for the fact that the Creator has taken upon Himself the effects of evil and has personally experienced what is impossible for any of us to endure. This is most important! When the question of "Where is God?" is asked, the answer of Jesus' life and death is: "right in the middle of this suffering," and He is experiencing it beyond what any other human could feel.

Therefore His allowing evil takes on a very personal cast. In graphic terms, every expression of evil (which He has sovereignly permitted) is like pulling down on the nailed hands and feet, grinding the raw back into the wood of the Cross. It does not matter if it is my sin, your sin, or even nature chaotically striking out, the incarnation of God into the flesh means that He now is suffering even more because of it. Perhaps, sometimes when we wonder why God is not answering us in our pain, it is because we do not hear *His* groans as He is no mere sympathetic bystander, but rather actually, personally taking on our suffering.

Keeping the End in Sight

Years ago, this writer pondered why in "the New Birth" and in "the New Creation" of Baptism, why does the Lord not just make us perfect immediately? Think of all the struggles, embarrassments, failures, deliberate sins/rebellions that would never have happened in our lives. It would be so simple, clean and final – we would have *arrived* at the threshold of heaven.

12

Most obviously God does not do that, but if He is neither helpless nor capricious, then to what purpose does He not? Clearly He has no urgency as He purifies and perfects: He chooses to use our *whole* lives to encompass this work, perhaps seventy or even a hundred years' worth – in fact, he seems to count as necessary the struggles, the embarrassments, the failures, and even the deliberate sins. No, not until our bodies (as well as all Creation) are recreated new on the Last Day will such "perfection" be finally achieved. However, we have received "the down payment" (or "the earnest" [II Corinthians 1:22; 5:5 KJV]) of the Holy Spirit to confirm that this final purification is indeed coming. So could the Lord be declaring that there is a greater "good(s)" presently at work than this moment's happiness and satisfaction?

Part of the answer lies in how we are (still) a key pivot in Creation's ability to glimpse its Creator. Even in how we use His resources of forgiveness, help, discipline, and more, others and perhaps even the *cosmos* get to see that these very gifts are for them as well. Also when *we* are baffled at what Jehovah is doing, they can discover that neither will *their* uncertainty condemn them. We, who are at the same level in which they live and not even close to perfect, still can reveal the Rock of Salvation to which we cling – we have the occasion to "give an answer to all who ask you to account for the hope which is in you" [I Peter 3:15].

On the other hand, more than mere spectators and/or victims in this universe; by the Holy Spirit's power, we are partners and participants as Jehovah overcomes evil and Satan. The battleground may range from personal victory within ourselves (for example, temptation, personal suffering), to victory within our lives and community (for example, feeding the hungry, clothing the naked, sheltering the homeless), to victory within the world (for example, stopping despotic abuse as in World War II, diminishing the effects of famine, rebuilding after natural disasters), and who knows just how far our reach into all Creation goes. We do this high honor not as perfect beings but precisely as fallen and redeemed creatures, bearing witness as to just what our Lord can do with such as His People.

We also know that this does not exhaust His victories. There will be a final one where the Creator will step in and compel all things to be made right in the end. Then finally will be completed the development and preparation which our Lord has felt necessary; and not individually alone, but as His People we will enter into the position prepared for us, at Jesus' side as He reigns – and we co-reign with and in Him. Then will be put to rest the agony of Creation (of which St Paul speaks) who awaits this revealing of the children of God – an existence which is built not upon despair but on *hope* [Romans 8:19-21].

A Word About Faith

It is worthwhile to establish an understanding to a very basic concept in this discussion: faith. We seem to have the idea that faith, especially spiritual faith, is complicated, however it actually is quite simple. In fact, much of our lives constantly involves faith. In the Assisted Living residence where I have worked, at the meal times, the people go to the tables in the dining room. There is no second thought, they just go with the expectation of being fed – but what is happening is that they are responding to a promise that their meals would be provided. Should they be asked to describe where in their lives they use faith, this kind of very common example would probably never even cross their minds, yet it is faith nonetheless.

Should they call the doctor to make an appointment and are told "Next Wednesday at 1 o'clock." They hang up and their life is changed: transportation must be arranged, perhaps they must bathe beforehand, appropriate clothes must be chosen, the kitchen may be asked to prepare their meal a little early – in a variety of ways life is altered simply because a voice on the telephone made a promise. When using money at a store, when driving and coming to a green or a red light, even the TV guide – all have implied promises which we depend on in faith, all the time. Each promise calls forth from us the response of faith, and more, also the actions that result from that faith.

This is what St James speaks of when he says, "... faith by itself, if it has no have works, is dead. ... I from my works will show you the faith" [James 2:17-18]: choices are made, courses of action are determined, Life – and living – is altered because of a promise.

So how is spiritual faith different than common, everyday faith? It is not in the method, but in the object of faith: our struggle is not so much in what God says, that is, "the promises," instead it lies in believing *the Promiser*. Ever since Adam and Eve, we have not been sure that we can trust Him. We really suspect that He does not want the best for us; and even if He did, He is basically helpless against the evil which seems to overwhelm us. We grapple with whether God really will make good on what He pledges. This attitude is both the cause [Genesis 3] and the result of our rebellion.

Rebellion and suspicion are so entrenched into human nature, there is no way on our own we would have confidence in His Word. It requires inside help from an outside Source: "no one can say that Jesus is Lord except by the Holy Spirit" [I Corinthians 12:3]. We have the Holy Spirit and therefore what lies before us is to grow in this confidence in the Lord. Faith is built upon promises, so to increase faith is to go and discover what He has pledged and what it means. The other half is to build up our confidence in the Promiser, so it is important (through the Holy Spirit) to watch how He operates and most importantly *why* He does what He does.

15

Suffering Faith

Often faith can be such a normal part of life, that when there are no "bells and whistles," that is, no dramatic, profound, or emotional experiences to highlight it, we may question whether we have it at all, which in the spiritual arena can create a very big distress. In response, we need only look at how our life has been affected in our attitudes, perspectives, feelings, methods, schedules, what we will or will not do, what we will or will not say, promises to which we hold, and many other things which show a difference from the usual of the world around us. This is what St James is saying in his quote above: "I from my works will *show you* the faith."

But there are also times when we argue and wrestle with Jehovah, we fight and are so frustrated with Him, and we wonder whether we are losing our faith. We see promises which seem wonderfully meant for others, and yet are so empty for us. We feel as though the door has been slammed in our faces. We can understand how Jacob feels the night before his reunion with his brother, as he spends the night wrestling with, in essence, God, [Genesis 32:24-32] and ends up the worse for wear: his hip is thrown out of joint! In the end, not everything would be back to the way it was: every step afterwards would likely have a twinge of pain – a limp [v 31] – in his life. But in desperation he refuses to let go without a blessing – and he gets it: he and his brother are graciously reunited. The limp would be the badge, the reminder of how much he *really* wanted his brother back, yet also the reminder of how – as the thigh was put out of joint – the separation between the brothers had not been necessary if they had just relied on the Lord's direction of their lives [see Genesis 27].

No, we are not losing our faith when we wrestle with God. Otherwise why would we even expend the energy? We would simply dismiss Him and walk away. After all, what is there of which to be convinced, if He is no

16

longer part of the picture? But we struggle, holding on for that blessing, trying to makes sense with how He and His promises fit into what often is the confusing puzzle of life – we are taking seriously His place in the picture, we *want* Him to be with us and we want to know it. Sometimes though, in the struggle something in our life also gets "put out of joint" – however, it is but a reminder of our earnest desire in grappling with God.

In contrast, at the Cross we also discover not the abandonment of God , but in our great surprise His answer, "I will not let *you* go, and – I – will bless you!" Here is ultimately revealed His heart, to which we desperately hold even when bewildered at the collapse of everything which we have held dear. In Holy Communion, He binds Himself to us to where He cannot back down nor back out. He cannot avoid being a literal part of us; He cannot avoid going with us in our body and in our heart as vividly as the bread and wine become one with us. He cannot avoid being part, yes, even of our struggles with His promises. He cannot avoid standing with us at the utter devastation of the Cross, but then also as He leads us on to the Resurrection with its power and its life.

2. Life and Pain

Death

It is important to establish a definition and description of death in order to make sense of its relationship to pain. A useful illustration in this regard is that of the deep sea diver in the old fashioned bell helmet with the air hose running up to an air pump on the surface of the water.

The deeper the diver goes, the more pressure is required to get the air down to him, particularly because otherwise the hose would collapse. However, that very life-saving substance (air) also makes the hose more and more rigid. The diver becomes more and more restricted as he investigates deeper into the shipwreck since the hose is reluctant to bend around corners, as well as it becomes quite "a drag" to pull through the passageways.

Finally the diver reaches the maximum where he can go. Yet he "just knows" the treasure which he seeks is just a little farther. In frustration and desperation, he whips out his knife and severs the hose from the helmet. Yes, now he has the freedom he seeks to pursue his "treasure." But he is a fool, for from the moment he cuts the lifeline, even though he may have ten to fifteen minutes of air in his suit, he actually is a walking dead man. And he will experience the foretastes of that decision, as he experiences low oxygen, high carbon dioxide saturation, suffocation, panic, and perhaps the agony of realizing just how meaningless has been his action.

This is what humanity has done in regard to its lifeline with its Creator. In rebellion the connection has been broken, and even though Methuselah could live 969 years, yet from his birth he is a dead man. Nobody gets out of this world alive (except, of course, those who are alive when Jesus returns[7]). Well, all right, two did, Enoch and Elijah, although some believe that they will return at the end times as the two witnesses of Revelation 11 and will also have their day – or death – as well. It is well to note that not even God the Son, when He comes into flesh, does not "get out" without first facing death, even though it is by His choice.

For all the rest of us, the process of dying begins from the moment we are born. But this is more than just physical death. It is to be cut off from the Lord; it is to *prefer* an existence broken from Him. Unless something diverts the obvious and natural outcome, the culmination of this is Hell, the final confirmation of a rebellion which demands to be without God.

As an aside, there have been some who have praised Adam and Eve for "thinking for themselves" – which has about as much wisdom behind it as the foolish deep sea diver had. If the diver truly did apply intelligence to his desire, he would have realized that there were far better other ways by which to reach his goal rather than being disconnected from his only source of life. However, a different way might require more patience and commitment, or he may finally conclude that the goal was just not worth the cost – that is the *real* "thinking for oneself," rather than simply a "knee-jerk" glorifying of rebellion. Still God allows even *that* prerogative.

But no matter now. The deed has been done. The problem is what is to be done about it.

The Lord from Heaven to Earth Descends

That very evening Jehovah shows up at Adam and Eve's "doorstep." This does not seem really all that unusual, since God enjoys His partnership with humans – that is why He created them! It is just like He comes one day to visit Abraham [Genesis 18], whom James calls "the friend of God" [2:23]; and He talks with Moses "face-to-face as with a friend" [Exodus 33:11; see Numbers 12:8].

But this time it is different – this couple are hiding from Him, knowing that their rebellion deserves the penalty of which they have been forewarned: "you shall surely die." Here is their first pain, a spiritual one: they discover they are naked, vulnerable, exposed. We think of physical death, but likely it is the discovery of an extraordinary loneliness and emptiness they have never experienced before. They face an overwhelming Creation isolated from its Creator. They face a human nature which is now marked by rebellion in every direction: "we have gone each our own way" [Isaiah 53:6].

God demands something painful from them: He calls them to account and seeks a confession of their sin. They are all too eager to blame someone else, even God Himself, but finally they do admit that they ate of the forbidden tree. The Lord delivers His sentence: not a curse, but rather that pain will now be their lifetime companion – He "turns up the pain."

Pain and Death

To the woman He said: "I will greatly increase your toil/pain in your childbearing; in pain/sorrow you shall bring forth children; your longing shall be for your husband, and he shall rule over you."
Then to Adam He said, "Because you have given heed to your wife, and have eaten from the tree of which I commanded you, saying, 'You shall not eat of it': Bound/cursed is the ground because of you; in toil/pain you shall eat of it all the days of your life; thorns and thistles[8] it shall bring forth for you and you shall eat of cultivated plants. By the sweat of your face you shall eat bread until you return to the ground, for out of it you were taken; you are dust, and to dust you shall return."…
Genesis 3:16-19

As the fallen humans stand before "the Judge of all the earth" [Genesis 18:25], He indicates that through their rebellion something new has infected Creation: death with its heralds, "toil" and "pain." "Toil" was once defined as when work, which can be pleasurable, because of the press of time or volume or whatever the stress is, is marked by fatigue, drudgery, and anxiousness – when it no longer is enjoyable, yet still must be done –, now it becomes *toil*. The Hebrew word encompasses this idea of "toil" along with "pain," and the Creator indicates that the existences both of the man and of the woman will now be marked by these odors of death, particularly in the most fundamental aspects of their lives.

For the woman, the joy of childbirth and the exhilaration of bringing life into the world will now include these reminders, with the possibility of even death itself entering in. The man, once God's leader for Creation, will instead find it rising up in rebellion against this rebel. Rather than a responsive and cooperative universe, he will see the destruction of his toil in droughts, floods, hailstorms, windstorms, tornadoes and earthquakes; he will watch his crops be devastated by weeds, disease and insects; he will experience famines, epidemics and "bad genes."

"Bound/cursed is the ground": rudderless, drifting and decaying, even Creation itself is marked by the odors of death:

> For Creation was subjected to aimlessness and corruption, not voluntarily, but because of Him Who subjected it in hope; because the Creation also will be freed from the slavery of corruption into the freedom of the Glory of the children of God. For we know that the whole Creation groans and travails together until now. Romans 8:20-22

So, although not directly causing the hurricane or tsunami, yet humanity's continued rebellion against Jehovah lies at the root of the catastrophes that plague our *cosmos* – because when creation looks even to *us*, there is no clear image of its Creator by which to regain its balance.

Where then is God in all this? Is He a petulant sadist, merely standing by, satisfied in mankind's pain and toil according to the sentence He has pronounced? What really is the mission of these harbingers of death upon humanity?

Pain: The Gift Nobody Wants

Pain: The Gift Nobody Wants is the original name of a book Dr Paul Brand co-authored with Philip Yancey (it has been republished under the name, *The Gift of Pain*). The doctor had spent his lifetime working with lepers in India and then also in the United States. He came to understand that leprosy's greatest effect on the human body is not disfigurement (which is caused by secondary infections) but rather how it attacks the nerves which feel pain. He began to realize that pain is a wonderful and necessary warning system which demands attention, simply because something is wrong, sometimes terribly wrong, in fact may even be lethally wrong.

Although medicines can control and cure leprosy, the ability to feel pain never returns. Scratching and accidentally gouging the chin, using a shovel with a splintered handle or with a nail sticking out, failing to blink when there is something in the eye, stepping on a tack, even a fellow who wakes up to discover that a rat has been chewing on his hand – all situations where pain should alert the person to take immediate action, but the signal is never sent to the brain. If proper care is not taken for the injury, infection sets in, gangrene can follow, and the result may be such things as the destruction of facial features, deformed limbs, blindness, amputations, and even death.

At first Dr Brand thought of pain as God's one great mistake, but he gradually came to realize that it is an amazing feat of engineering. The sensors are not distributed randomly but rather are placed in clusters according to the needs of each area of the body. Thus the foot, the torso, the eye will interpret a firm tap at different levels of painfulness. Since diabetes and drug abuse can affect the ability to feel pain, he was asked by the US Public Health Service to design a replica of this warning system for those who have been so afflicted. Five years later, the project was abandoned.

A warning system suitable for just one hand was exorbitantly expensive, subject to frequent mechanical breakdown and hopelessly inadequate to interpret the mass of sensations the hand encounters. The system sometimes called "God's great mistake" was far too complex for even the most sophisticated technology to mimic. Philip Yancey[10]

But the largest problem was that if the warning signal was too mild, it would be ignored, and if it was too insistent, it would be turned off or taken off by the patient – thereby rendering the system useless.

What proved most daunting to his team, though, were those who *did* feel pain and it just didn't matter:

> I think the thing that finally convinced us we could not win was the study of patients with congenital indifference to pain. These children have intact nerves. They know what pressures they are experiencing but to them pain is not unpleasant. So they laugh at it and destroy themselves.
>
> I can still see the horror on a mother's face when she told me about her baby girl. This baby had just grown her first four teeth and the mother came in to find her laughing and gurgling with pleasure at a new game. She had bitten off the tip of her finger and was playing with the blood and making patterns with the drips. As we followed this child, we found later that she had enough nerves to know when things were sharp or when they were hot and she even learned to a certain extent to take care. But because pain was not unpleasant she only took note of it when it was convenient. Paul Brand[11]

He also noted how the societies who have progressed the most in controlling pain are also the least equipped to deal with it:

> The average Indian villager knows suffering well, expects it, and accepts it as an unavoidable challenge of life. In a remarkable way the people of India have learned to control pain at the level of the mind and spirit, and have developed endurance that we in the West find hard to understand. Westerners, in contrast, tend to view suffering as an injustice or failure, an infringement on their guaranteed right to happiness. Paul Brand[12]

In fact, as a counterpoint: the society which "conquers" pain finds that "pleasure" becomes too commonplace. As the emphasis and demands on pleasure therefore are constantly increased, contentment equally continues to be more elusive. How much does this attitude generate even more mental and emotional suffering, since the increasingly mythogical "satisfaction," which often breeds unrealistic expectations of other *human* beings, litters our lives with relationship after relationship cast aside because each just does not "measure up"? Pain is often necessary for us to finally realize, in what is too often our spiritually sense-deadened culture, what pleasure and joy really involve.

> Lin Yutang in his book *My Country and My People* tells of the ancient Chinese philosophy of happiness. He gives a list of the greatest pleasures of life. I was startled to find that in every one pain and ecstasy were inescapably mixed together. "To be dry and thirsty in a hot and dusty land – and to feel great drops of rain on my bare skin – ah, is that not happiness!" … Clearly, many ecstasies were withheld from those who have never suffered thirst or itch.   Paul Brand [13]

Dr Brand understood that pain, particularly chronic pain, can itself destroy a person's strength, and mental and emotional capacities. Yet if he could eradicate pain from the world, he would not do it. It is too valuable in preserving life. In the crossroads which pain creates, we are urged to turn from the path of danger and death, and to discover joy and value on the path which leads to life.

"I will Greatly Increase Your Toil/Pain …"

So says Jehovah to Eve as well to Adam in the context of Genesis 3. Had Dr Brand been consulted whether the Creator should "turn up the pain," knowing what he does about its function, likely he would have applauded the move. After all, pain is not so much a punishment but rather, primarily, the warning that something is terribly wrong – possibly even lethally wrong.

Often pain comes as a shock, a surprise, often catching us off guard – we are not prepared for its demand and suddenly we come face-to-face with our vulnerability; in chronic pain, its insistent encroachment on life makes our helplessness stand out. In fact, even in sickness – or as it used to be called, "infirmity", that is, weakness or feebleness – there is the irony of a tiny organism which inflicts such distress, even death, in a comparatively huge creature.

These are but foretastes of mortality since death is the ultimate weakness – when one has died, he can do nothing: he cannot get up, he cannot move an arm, he cannot even blink an eyelid. And for the most part, in three to four generations most people are completely forgotten except for perhaps as a vague name listed somewhere.

This is, of course, the reality for a humanity which wishes to become "like God," to usurp His position, and have cut themselves off from the Source of their life. This desire has descended throughout the generations and betrays itself in something so basic as when we make an important decision. We get stressed if we feel that there is some information which has eluded us – we want omniscience (all knowledge), even if in this case in a limited scope. We feel uneasy in regard to whether we are wise enough to choose the best alternative – we want perfect wisdom. We make a decision and then deride ourselves when something happens, "if only I had known …" – we want foreknowledge. Even when we have made "the correct choice," we have no power to control others or circumstances to compel them to conform – we want omnipotence (all power). The list goes on. And, broken from God, we just become more and more aware of how deep our inadequacies run.

Pain, frustration, spiritual isolation and death – "you are dust, and to dust you shall return" – is the reminder that unless we are connected with the Source of Life, all that remains of us is merely dust.

One of the possible Hebrew root words for pain (*'atsab*) provides a contrast descriptive of what has occurred in Genesis 3: on one hand, Job uses this word to speak of Jehovah: "Your hands have made me and fashioned me, an intricate unity …" [10:8]; yet also the word speaks of what *humans* fashion: idols [Jeremiah 44:19; Psalm 115:3-11]. It certainly is suggestive in view of the discussion so far. How much pain have we caused ourselves because we have fashioned idols, particularly of ourselves? Indeed, pain is not a contradiction of life; rather it is the call to return to life:

> … "Thus says the Lord Jehovah: "Repent, turn away from your idols; turn your faces away from all your abominations." …
> "Say to them: 'As I live,' says the Lord Jehovah, 'I do not delight in the death of the wicked, but that the wicked turn back from his way and live. Turn, turn from your evil ways! For why should you die…'
> Ezekiel 14:6; 33:11

So Jehovah "turns up the pain" in order to create a nagging warning that there is something dreadfully wrong in our world, in our culture, and in our lives. Yet we are so intent on "managing our pain" that we really are not listening, and instead vainly attempt to increase our pleasure to sooth and insulate us from the reality against which God (and pain) warns us – we want to turn off and take off this system of unrelenting irritation.

Leprosy

From Dr Brand's description of leprosy, one can understand why it is the one disease which God highlights in the Bible. The parallel to a "spiritual leprosy" is recognizable, and so, as the Creator "turns up the pain," humanity embarks on whatever method it can to kill sensitivity to the anguish.

Already in Genesis 3 the process has begun. Adam, in his "confession," prefaces it by blaming the Creator for giving him this woman and the woman for giving him the fruit – although he does admit having eaten of it on his own (she has not crammed it down his throat). Throughout history, "It's not my fault" has echoed until the modern age where it now has a more sophisticated tone to it. Via such things as psychology, we now have good reason to blame our parents, or the environment, or genes, or society, or drugs, or youth, or age, or … – all of which, like Adam and Eve's temporary façade (fig leaves, which dry up and crumble away), seek to cover and divert attention from the pain.

We attempt to avoid the spiritual torment of guilt by depicting Jehovah more as a blind, deaf old Grandfather Who merely pats us on our head as He passes by. Or else we just eliminate Him completely, as the theory of evolution attempts to do, and convince ourselves that there is no such thing as accountability. Yet all the time, there is a reality which each day relentlessly creeps closer and closer.

The Reality of Eternal Death

No matter how we attempt to avoid the pain, we end up just as deformed and damaged spiritually as the physical leprosy can do to the body, even to the point of spiritual death as well. Christopher Townsend, in his essay, "Hell: a difficult doctrine we dare not ignore" remarks:

> Generally, today, the possibility of hell is evaded rather than examined, or mocked as a relic of bygone beliefs or, in the world of literature, reinterpreted as a metaphor for the bitterness of the human condition. The irony is that the underlying intellectual trends which have undermined the credibility of divine judgement have also eroded confidence in the possibility of finding a shared morality or an authentic source of meaning for human life. Christopher Townsend[14]

As Dr Brand discovered, insensitivity is a two-way street: not only does it make one less able to realize the danger one is in, but it also empties the substance and the contentment of life. The person who refuses to acknowledge God's warning signals particularly concerning the spiritual threats facing him (and then to be drawn to the life which is eternal), is also a person who really has no purpose or value to his present existence, except merely to exist. The disease is in a most grave state, as Martin Luther describes (in regard to Holy Communion):

> If therefore, you are heavy-laden and feel your weakness, then go joyfully to this Sacrament and obtain refreshment, consolation, and strength...
>
> But if you say: What, then, shall I do if I cannot feel such distress or experience hunger and thirst for the Sacrament? Answer: For those who are so minded that they do not realize their condition, I know no better counsel than that they put their hand into their bosom to ascertain whether they also have flesh and blood. And if you find that to be the case, then go, for your good, to St. Paul's Epistle to the Galatians, and hear what sort of a fruit your flesh is: [chap. 5, 19ff.] ...
>
> Therefore, if you cannot feel it, at least believe the Scriptures, they will not lie to you and they know your flesh better than you yourself... But that we do not feel it is so much the worse; for it is a sign that this is a leprous flesh which feels nothing, and yet [the leprosy] rages and keeps spreading. Yet as we have said, if you are quite dead to all sensibility, still believe the Scriptures, which pronounce sentence upon you. And, in short, the less you feel your sins and infirmities, the more reason have you to go to the Sacrament to seek help and a remedy. Martin Luther[15]

Why should there be such concern? Because the danger is real and it is very final.

In the New Testament, where the prospects of heaven and hell are delineated, the standard term for 'hell' is gehenna [Footnote: Occasionally hades (especially Luke 16:23) and tartaroo (2 Peter 2:4) are translated as hell, but these terms appear to denote the intermediate state between death and final destiny]. It referred, in the first instance, to the Valley of Hinnom, south of Jerusalem which was notorious for child sacrifices offered to Molech (2 Chronicles 28:3), and later where Jerusalem's refuse was burned. In the light of prophetic warnings

(Jeremiah 7:30-3) it became a symbol for the eschatological fire of judgment.. ...

The New Testament speaks of hell as a place, the 'lake of fire' into which, after the dead are raised, the unrighteous and even Hades are thrown. [Revelation 20:14-15] However, it is a 'place' originally made for spirit beings [Matthew 25:41] ... In the age to come, the focal point of the universe is Christ on his throne, and around him the elect gathered from all the nations, in the new heaven and earth. Hell, though not 'nowhere', is utterly 'elsewhere'. Indeed, some have speculated that hell will be barely discernible: 'a speck upon the infinite azure of eternity'. [W.G.T. Shedd, *Dogmatic Theology* (Edinburgh: T. & T. Clark, 1889), Vol.II, p.745]   Christopher Townsend[16]

If indeed the Creator intended humans to be partners with Him forever, filling our future with meaning, purpose and usefulness – to "'jointly reign' with Him" [II Timothy 2:11-12] –, then Hell is the emptiness in contrast to all that. When one chooses to remain in his brokenness from God, then that severed relationship will remain forever.

There are only two kinds of people in the end: those who say to God, "Thy will be done," and those to whom God says, in the end, "Thy will be done." All that are in Hell, choose it. Without that self-choice there could be no Hell. No soul that seriously and constantly desires joy will ever miss it. Those who seek find. To those who knock it is opened.
                                                                          CS Lewis[17]

The Lepers

As He entered a certain village, there met Him ten men, lepers, who stood afar off. Lifting their voices, they called, "Jesus, Master, have mercy on us!"

Perceiving [their need], He said to them, "Go your way, and show yourselves to the priests." And it happened that in their going to them, they were cleansed.

But one of them, perceiving that he was healed, turned back with a loud voice glorifying God, and fell on his face at His feet, giving Him thanks – and he was a Samaritan!

Jesus in response said, "Were not ten cleansed – where are the nine? Were not found any who returned to give God glory except this foreigner?" He said to him, "Arise, go your way. Your faith has made you well."   Luke 17:12-19

Based on the discussion so far, it is easy to see both kinds of leprosy at work. Although the physical ailment is cured, the spiritual insensitivity remains in the nine. The warning pain never has made it into the spiritual consciousness. Now that the illness is no longer a problem, normal life is to be resumed with its goal a supposed "contentment."

But there is one, a most unlikely one, whose spiritual sensitivities are a bit keener perhaps because he is a despised Samaritan, and the message of the pain achieves its purpose: this human is reunited with his God.

There is another time when the pain calls the sufferer out from humanity's common rebellion and into humility and faith:

> Behold, a leper came and worshiped Him, saying, "Lord, if You are willing, You have power to cleanse me."
> Stretching out His hand, Jesus touched him, saying, "I am willing; be cleansed." Immediately his leprosy was cleansed.   Matthew 8:2-3

The point though is not simply to identify the types of leprosy, but rather that because of the One Who has come to share not only our humanity but also the realities of our existence – "Surely He has borne our calamities and carried our agonies" [Isaiah 53:4] – in Him there is healing to be found. As we will discuss, Jehovah does not often operate on our timetable, yet He will apply His compassion and healing to where we need it the most, both inside us as well as on the outside.

His Own Medicine

After the Creator tells the rebels that He will "turn up the pain," He does something which contrasts against any thought that He is motivated by vindictiveness: for those who have experienced the anguish of the nakedness and emptiness of their lives; for those who have felt vulnerable and afraid before a Creation no longer their friend; for those who now experience the tastes of death which will dog their heels every day throughout their lifetimes – *He clothes them.*

But this is not some mere fashion statement: *God* now *chooses* – the skins have come from a victim of His choice, an innocent victim who sheds its blood so that human nakedness, vulnerability, and rebellion could be covered. This is the first in a long line of sacrifices which point to a more excellent solution to come, when "The Lamb of God, Who takes away the sin of the world" [John 1:29] ascends a Cross to provide the perfect and eternal solution for those, who like the two lepers above, have also realized their *spiritual* leprosy.

When God gives His creatures the right to choose "to not love," He does not violate His commitment to allowing this choice, but He will declare to them the spiritual reality which awaits the rebellious ones: they will have foretastes of eternal death and hell (that eternal culmination of being broken from the Creator) which are to call them back to life. But one thing more He does – He Himself comes in Person, in Jesus, to walk among humans and to plead with them [Luke 13:34; also the Parable of the Vineyard tenants, Mark 12:1:12], as He joins them in the pain of this existence:

> Because God came and took a place besides us, he fully understands. Dorothy Sayers says:
>
>> For whatever reason God chose to make man as he is – limited and suffering and subject to sorrows and death – He had the honesty and courage to take His own medicine. Whatever game He is playing with His creation, He has kept His own rules and played fair. He can exact nothing from man that He has not exacted from Himself. He has Himself gone through the whole of human experience, from the trivial irritations of family life and the cramping restrictions of hard work and lack of money to the worst horrors of pain and humiliation, defeat, despair and death. When He was a man, He played the man. He was born in poverty and

died in disgrace and thought it well worthwhile (*Christian Letters to a Post-Christian World*, Eerdmans, 1969, p. 14).

By taking it on himself, Jesus in a sense dignified pain. Of all the kinds of lives he could have lived, he chose a suffering one.   Philip Yancey[18]

It is in this common experience of pain and suffering, He speaks of purpose to the pain; but more, *He stands in the middle of it with us*, in every step of the way from conception to death, and then demonstrates that there is a resurrection – and all of this to bring willing humans back into an indescribable relationship with Him which will span eternity, never to be broken again:

> The Spirit Himself witnesses with our spirit that we are God's children, and if children, then heirs: indeed God's heirs and joint-heirs with Christ, provided we jointly suffer in order that we may also be jointly glorified. For I conclude that the sufferings of this present time are not worthy in light of the Glory about to be revealed in us. For in earnest expectation, Creation expectantly awaits the revealing of the sons of God.   Romans 8:16-19

3. Submission

Ravensbruck

"Corrie!" she said excitedly. "He's given us the answer! Before we asked, as He always does! In the Bible this morning. Were was it? Read that part again!"

... "It was in First Thessalonians," I said. ... In the feeble light I turned the pages. "Here it is: 'Comfort the frightened, help the weak, be patient with everyone. See that none of you repays evil for evil, but always seek to do good to one another and to all ...'" It seemed written expressly to Ravensbruck.

"Go on," said Betsie. "That wasn't all."

"Oh yes: '... to one another and to all. Rejoice always, pray constantly, give thanks in all circumstance; for this is the will of God in Christ Jesus – "

"That's it, Corrie! That's His answer. 'Give thanks in all circumstances!' That's what we can do. We can start right now to thank God for every single thing about this new barracks!"

... "Such as?" I said.

"Such as being assigned here together."

I bit my lip. "Oh yes, Lord Jesus!"

... I looked down at the Bible. "Yes! Thank You, dear Lord ... Thank You for all the women, here in this room, who will meet You in these pages."

"Yes," said Betsie. "Thank You for the very crowding here. Since we're packed so close, that many more will hear!" She looked at me expectantly. "Corrie!" she prodded.

"Oh, all right. Thank You for the jammed, crammed, stuffed, packed, suffocating crowds."

"Thank You," Betsie went on serenely, "for the fleas and for – "

The fleas! This was too much. "Betsie, there's no way even God can make me grateful for a flea."

"'Give thanks in *all* circumstances,'" she quoted. "It doesn't say, 'in pleasant circumstances.' Fleas are part of this place where God has put us."

And so we stood between piers of bunks and gave thanks for fleas. But this time I was sure Betsie was wrong.   Corrie ten Boom[19]

In the book *The Hiding Place*, Corrie ten Boom many times wonders of what sort of creature her sister is. She does not seem to be someone from this plane of existence. Rather, it seems as though Betsie has one foot firmly placed in heaven.

The gates of Ravensbruck would strike fear into the hearts of all who enter – the dark smoke from the tall chimneys indicates that for the vast majority there is but one way out, and no trace will be left of one's life other than a ledger number with a name attached. Of all the other ways by which the prisoners are degraded into a non-human status, it seems like the last straw to be assigned to a barracks terribly infested with fleas.

And now Betsie insists that they should be thankful even for fleas. What is worse, it is one thing to give thanks for fleas for the moment, it is quite another to "give thanks" for the fleas day after day.

"Did Your God of Love Will This?"

In the movie version, "Maria" challenges Betsie's seeming fantasy idealism with the skepticism of harsh realities, of hands broken by hard work, of near starvation rations, of inadequate protection against the biting cold of winter, and of the stench of the ever-present chimneys.

"Did your God of Love will this?" she cries out. And really can she be blamed? The pedigree of the question is ancient. The sharpest example is when the Magi leave and Joseph hurries his family to Egypt, we look at the deaths of the innocent children and immediately cry out, "how could God?!"

Here is a spiritual *pain* which insists on an answer – something is wrong, something extremely wrong – the nerve endings are on overload. It is a range grass fire which burns off the deceptive façades, exposing what really lies underneath – all self-indulgent descriptions of the meaning of life are stripped away and leaving – leaving what? Is there anything that can respond to this pain with an answer that has substance?

Hypocrisy

Yet is there not a bit of hypocrisy in the background of Maria's question? Humans want the luxury of "free will," but if one is not allowed to exercise it, then just how "free" can it be? We want "free will" but then we blame the Creator whenever it turns out badly – as if to say, "How dare He give us such an unbridled freedom!"

Maybe it should be a "partial" free will – but how can that be truly "free"? And who will determine whether the impact of *this* kind of action to *this* degree is permissible, but anything beyond *that* degree is not allowed? However, the consequences may be subtle, for example, in gradually eroding another person's self-confidence, so that at first things do not seem so bad and yet as time goes on the results are devastating. One would be hard pressed to find a rebellion against God that does not affect "innocent" people in some negative way, whether immediately or in the future – Abraham's forcing the birth of a son [Ishmael – Genesis 16:1-6] creates a problem which brings anguish for the world some four thousand years later in the Arab and Israeli conflict. Even a road to self-destruction will have victims among family and friends, with ripples touching other lives.

How satisfying it would be to dictate to the Creator what is and is not permissible to our sensibilities, to be His master and override His wisdom, methods and goals! Why could God not have done it this way, or that way, so that we are not stuck with this result? Satan's "For God knows ..." [Genesis 3:5] insinuates that the Lord does know better, but is selfishly holding back on what should rightfully be ours. The movie "Bruce Almighty" wrestles with this theme, where "Bruce" is given God's job for a week, and even at that short a stint and dealing with not the whole world (much less the *cosmos*) but only with the Buffalo, New York area, he ends up realizing that the task is beyond his capacity. It identifies how we want to dictate acceptable outcomes, but ultimately we are driven to God for Him to do the job, since He alone is adequately equipped – and then He is criticized for doing the job.

On the other hand, in Times Square in New York City, there is a little "Ripley's Believe It or Not" museum which has an exhibit of medieval torture items. It is appalling to see the human creativity and capacity at causing suffering in a fellow human. Yet this covers but a small slice of the history of evoking pain and agony. Even today things have not really changed except perhaps in our sophistication: not only are there machete massacres, now we can text-bully on the iPhone; not only are there poachers excited by the higher prices of an endangered species, but there are corporate executives giving themselves bonuses for destroying millions of people's retirement investments; not only are there the office-politics' back-stabbings and character assassinations, but there are the "entertainment" industry's glorifying of treachery, selfishness and cruelty.

In the book *Peace Child*, missionaries and readers have been appalled at how in a primitive New Guinea culture, a person would work hard to win the confidence of someone, simply to set the other person up literally "for the kill." When they first heard the story of Judas' betrayal of Jesus, they cheered this "hero." Yet really how different is this from what is so often depicted in our "sophisticated" "reality shows"? Of course, it is the "survival of the fittest" and therefore it should be permissible: the weak are to be destroyed – which brings us back to the concentration camps.

No, it is not God Who holds the sword or the knife, it is not God with the finger on the trigger, it is not God Who stabs in the back, it is not God Who cheats others, it is not God Who disregards other people – it is the human being with the bloody hands. Walt Kelly's comic strip "Pogo" once made the famous comment, "we have met the enemy and they is us" – it *is* us. How hypocritical it is to blame God for the evils of the world, which are done by our mouths, our actions, our attitudes.

The real question is not "How could God …?" but rather "How could humans?!" As Corrie says in the movie, "God did not build this place; men did."

The Dark Side of Free Will

If the freedom to choose evil is to be given, then it must be wholly given, and the consequences are to be experienced in full, rather than only allowing a mere minor discomfort. How else will the terrible nature of sin be fully revealed? A parallel might be made in regard to an alcoholic or an addict of any kind – how often must they "hit bottom" before they realize the destructiveness of their addiction, how they have *submitted* the control of their lives to something that now dominates them, and therefore they need help? The "enabler" in these cases attempts to soften the blow for them, fix the problems and hide the results, but, rather than helping the addict, he simply gives implied permission to continue their destructive behavior by not allowing the outcomes and the responsibilities to be faced.

So then what should God do with the very real destructiveness of mankind's rebellion? sugar-coat everything in order to mute its results and responsibilities, or should He expose it in all of its "glory"? If God assumes the role of an enabler, how then can He effect the true rescue of mankind? The point of exposing suffering, such as a day honoring the innocents killed by Herod being placed in such proximity to the good feelings of Christmas, is to reveal just how close to the surface lie the unpleasant aspects of our rebellion (sin) against God. Yes, it is humans who have the blood on their hands (even on ours as well); mankind's freedom to choose and then to rebel against God has brought about so much suffering in our world.

39

However, in reverse, that Christmas should be placed so close to such horror is to identify what ultimately is the Creator's deep yearning for all humanity: as hopeless as the human cruelty can seem, He personally steps in to make available an answer. Suffering makes us understand not only the fragileness of our human character behind the saying, "there but for the grace of God, go I," but also the depth of commitment behind "for God so loved ... that He gave His only Son ..." [John 3:16].

In reply to Maria's challenge, Corrie admits that she cannot answer in regard to why the suffering that surrounds them has been allowed, but this she does know, that "this same God you are accusing came and lived in the midst of our world; He was beaten, and He was mocked, and He died on a Cross, and He did it for Love – for us."

> Sometimes I would slip the Bible from its little sack with hands that shook, so mysterious had it become to me. It was new; it had just been written. I marveled sometimes that the ink was dry. I had believed the Bible always, but reading it now had nothing to do with belief. It was simply a description of the way things were – of hell and heaven, of how men act and how God acts. I had read a thousand times the story of Jesus' arrest – how soldiers had slapped Him, laughed at Him, flogged Him. Now such happenings had faces and voices.   Corrie ten Boom[20]

Even as the women had to stand naked before their captors, they realized that Jesus was naked on the Cross – naked before *His* captors, naked as Adam and Eve had been before a no longer sympathetic Creation. Not only are we not abandoned, our Lord has directly involved Himself in *our* humanity, withholding nothing in His experiencing the full range of the human condition.

"To Be [a God] or Not To Be"

Begging Shakespeare's pardon, but really "that is the question." In attempting to grab the reigns from the Creator, we discover we are ill-equipped for the job and others are not so eager to go along with us. But most of us do not really want to rule the universe, we would be content to be gods at least within our large or small corner of the world. Being a god is like trying to keep items in a water-soaked box, things just keep breaking out, first here, then there. It is hard to always think ahead of all the possibilities that will affect us; it is frustrating since so much of our world is that over which we have absolutely no control; we are tired or too much has overwhelmed us. But how can we exert our will unless there are those who will follow us? We struggle to gain this power over others, whether by strength, influence, money, coercion, sex, or whatever it may take to make our will happen.

King Herod the Great provides a good, although extreme example of this. He has done everything he could to become the god of his corner of the Roman Empire. In his mind he is a benevolent god, providing beautiful buildings, especially a rebuilt temple for Jehovah, and doing other "good things" for his subjects. But the Jews do not want to play – they are not in agreement that he, a non-Jew, should have this power over them. His hold on the throne is tenuous. To maintain control he resorts to murder, and when faced even with the presence of Jehovah Himself, he pulls out the knife.

And there stands the "god" with the bloody hands, whether Herod or Pol Pot or Hitler or the Klu Klux Klan or the guy in the muscle-shirt who just gave his family a good pounding or the woman who has "stabbed in the back" someone who was in her way or the teenager who has a minute ago on his iPhone embarrassed "a wimp." No, it is not Jehovah's hands that are bloody, it is the hands of the humanity who thinks they could be gods on par with Him. When we want to fault "God" for the suffering in the world, perhaps we should be more clear as to which one we are referring to.

In contrast, Jehovah, the "real God," is left to clean up the muck from generations and millennia of these billions of "gods." This is what Christmas is about, as the Lord steps into our world with not a shovel, but with a Cross in hand. He carries the accumulation of century after century upon Himself; "For Christ died for sins once for all, the Righteous for the unrighteous, to bring you to God" [I Peter 3:18]; "He Himself is the Propitiation/atoning Sacrifice for our sins, and not for ours only but also for the whole world" [I John 2:2]. And that is why "the slaughter of the innocents" occurs in such proximity in both the Biblical account and in the Church year. Yes, the suffering is the warning that there is something wrong, lethally wrong in our world. But that birth in a stable and death on a Cross is the Good News that He takes care of the mess; and then through an empty tomb, an Ascension, and a coming return on the Last Day, a process has irretrievably begun which will culminate in "Behold I make all things new" [Revelation 21:5].

To think that still we complain when He does not do the job to our liking.

"To Obey Him"

Maria asks, "And why do you think your God of Love sent you here?" Betsy answers, "To obey Him."

What kind of an answer is that?! Maria – and we – demand something with enough substance to counteract the unavoidable harsh realities which surround us. We want a grand purpose, something that shows the suffering to be worthwhile. We want a hope to which to cling and to watch as it comes closer and closer. We want a reward which is guaranteed in writing. We want a down payment "in hand" so that we may be confident when all seems lost. We want proof that God is really on the ball and with us. But "to obey," to be given a *responsibility* – that certainly is not what we have in mind.

Yet there is purpose behind our being restored to that significant position before Creation for which mankind was created and to "co-reign" in Christ forever. We have the cross-bought final redemption which daily comes closer to us. It is all in writing, in God's diary of His heart and soul: the Bible. We have the "down payment" or the "earnest" of the Holy Spirit given through Baptism. We have the constant reaffirmation of His presence in and with us in Holy Communion, and in the presence of His Body, the Church. The Lord has done His part.

As the opening quote to this chapter describes, Corrie often is admittedly reluctant in the face of Betsy's enthusiasm to "obey" what "is the will of God in Christ Jesus for you." Yet she comes to realize that those fleas, for which she reluctantly but obediently has given thanks, are the protection which gives the women in their barracks the freedom and safety to discuss the Lord, without the horrors which other barracks experience. And one particular day she learns what the Creator can do with obedience, a story she has been fond to repeat:

One day after the war, after Corrie gave a talk in Germany about God's presence and forgiveness even in the midst of a concentration camp, "a former SS man who had stood guard at the shower room door in the processing center at Ravensbruck" came forward to express his gratefulness for the forgiveness of which she spoke. He offered his hand to her, but "suddenly it was all there – the roomful of mocking men, the heaps of clothing, Betsie's pain blanched face."

> Even as the angry, vengeful thoughts boiled through me, I saw the sin of them. Jesus Christ had died for this man; was I going to ask for more? Lord Jesus, I prayed, forgive me and help me to forgive him.
> I tried to smile, I struggled to raise my hand. I could not. ... And so again I breathed a silent prayer. Jesus, I cannot forgive him. Give me Your forgiveness.

As I took his hand the most incredible thing happened. From my shoulder along my arm and through my hand a current seemed to pass from me to him while into my heart sprang a love for this stranger that almost overwhelmed me.   Corrie ten Boom [21]

Walking in Them

We are His handiwork, created in Christ Jesus for good works, which God prepared previously that we should walk in them   Ephesians 2:10

What an astounding concept: God has already prepared everything for our lives – it does not require a lot of planning, nor effort, but simply to "walk"! This links with Jesus' words:

Come to Me, all you who toil to exhaustion and are burdened, and I will give you rest. Take My yoke upon you and disciple from Me, for I am humbly gentle and humble before God in heart, and you will find rest for your souls; for My yoke is suitable and useful, and My burden is easy to bear.   Matthew 11:28-30

Suffering makes us stand at a crossroad: it challenges us as to whether we come in struggle, rebellion and belligerence to God's plans, or whether we "disciple [learn]" from Jesus Who is "humbly gentle and humble before God in heart," finding His "yoke … suitable and useful" and His "burden … easy."

There are times when Corrie talks about some cruelty and her first reaction is concern for the victim. However, Betsy's first reaction is to pray for the perpetrator of the cruelty:

I seized Betsie's arm as the command to march came again, more to steady myself than her. … Such cruelty was too much to grasp, too much to bear. Heavenly Father, carry it for me! …
   "Betsie!" I wailed, " how long will it take?"
   "Perhaps a long, long time. Perhaps many years. But what better way could there be to spend our lives?"
   I turned to stare at her. "Whatever are you talking about?"

"These young women. That girl back at the bunkers. Corrie, if people can be taught to hate, they can be taught to love! We must find the way, you and I, no matter how long it takes ..."

She went on, almost forgetting in her excitement to keep her voice to a whisper, while I slowly took in the fact that she was talking about our guards. I glanced at the matron seated at the desk ahead of us. I saw a gray uniform and a visored hat; Betsie saw a wounded human being.

And I wondered, not for the first time what sort of a person she was, this sister of mine ... what kind of road she followed while I trudged beside her on the all-too-solid-earth.   Corrie ten Boom[22]

What puzzled me all this time was Betsie. She had suffered everything I had and yet she seemed to carry no burden of rage. .."Betsie, don't you feel anything about Jan Vogel? Doesn't it bother you?"

"Oh yes, Corrie! Terribly! I've felt for him ever since I knew – and pray for him whenever his name comes into my mind. How dreadfully he must be suffering!"

For a long time I lay silent ...Once again I had the feeling that this sister with whom I had spent all my life belonged somehow to another order of beings. Wasn't she telling me in her gentle way that I was as guilty as Jan Vogel? Didn't he and I stand together before an all-seeing God convicted of the same sin of murder? For I had murdered him with my heart and with my tongue.

"Lord Jesus," I whispered into the lumpy ticking of the bed, "I forgive Jan Vogel as I pray that You will forgive me. I have done him great damage. Bless him now, and his family ..." That night for the first time since our betrayer had a name I slept deep and dreamlessly until the whistle summoned us to roll call.   Corrie ten Boom[23]

Jesus had said:

You have heard that it was said, 'You shall love your neighbor and hate your enemy', but I say to you: Love your enemies, bless those who curse you, do nobly to those who hate you, and pray for those who abuse you and persecute you, that you may be sons of your Father in heaven; because He makes His sun rise on the evil and on the good, and sends rain on the righteous and on the unrighteous.   Matthew 5:43-45

Who are the "innocent"? Who are the "sufferers"? Who are the "just"? Who are the "unjust"? This is not to make light of those who suffer at the hands of cruelty, but Betsie does turn things around. *All of us* are sufferers.

All of us condemn others to suffering, perhaps not actively but by our lack of prayers for them, or by our lack of expressing God's Love toward them.

The burden is "easy to bear," the good works are "already prepared" – they really are not that complicated or hard to do – and yet we perpetuate the suffering, theirs and ours, because we are not "humbly gentle and humble before God in heart." Yes, we need to "disciple [learn]" from Jesus. Why are you here? "To obey Him," was Betsie's answer.

The Other Hypocrisy

This then enters the realm of "the other hypocrisy": in contrast to the hypocrisy about who holds "the bloody knife," what about the antiseptically clean hands?

The last Matthew quote identifies how our Lord's intention is to bring us full circle back to the reason why humanity was created in the first place: to be the Image of God, the reflection and demonstration of the Creator; to be the spiritual window through which the *cosmos* and all humanity can see and experience its Maker and His Glory. In Exodus 33:18-19, when asked to show His Glory, Jehovah emphasizes, not power, majesty or government, nor even the honor and the praise due Him, but instead He accents His goodness, Covenant relationship, grace, and mercy; then in 34:6-8, He adds His Steadfast Love, faithfulness, forgiveness and justice.

The New Testament continues the emphasis, as John declares, that in Jesus, "we have seen His Glory, Glory as of the only-begotten of the Father, full of grace and truth" [John 1:14]; and St Paul ties the Image of God to the Glory of God: "But we all, with unveiled face, beholding the Glory of the Lord as in a mirror, are being transformed into the same Image from glory to Glory, exactly as from the Lord the Spirit" [II Corinthians 3:18] – or as Jesus put it simply, "Come, follow Me."

46

Jehovah is inalterably committed to make mankind an essential sharer in not just His work but also in His delight and joy in these activities and accomplishments. Human participation is so essential that angels will not take up the slack, nor will God back down on His chosen dependence upon and trust in us. Not even the fall into sin releases humanity from its obligation, nor is this commission from the Creator a mere part-time role or recreational option.

The question, "Why did God not do anything about ...(for example, the concentration camps)?" therefore avoids the fact that after nineteen centuries of the influence of Jesus and the Holy Spirit, Jehovah can legitimately say that He has fully equipped humanity to stand against such things as the Nazi philosophy, and to stand against the cruelty that surfaced throughout those years. The real question then, is rather "Why did humans not do anything?" How many people knew but ignored the evidence? How many suspected but refused to find out? How many kept their hands "antiseptically clean"? How often has the choice – of even the nations – been one of reluctance, accommodation, sometimes even secret support, which allows evil to flourish, as in the case of the Second World War where it then requires six years of war to stop the unbridled evil.

The Light of God

> In Him has [always] been Life, and the Life has [always] been the Light of men. The Light shines in the darkness, and the darkness has [never] overcome It. ... This is the judgment: the Light has come into the world, and men have rather loved the darkness than the Light, since their works have been evil. For everyone who does evil hates the Light and does not come to the Light, lest his deeds might be exposed.
>
> John 1:4-5; 3:19-20

Would that being the Image which reflects the Glory of God were a comfortable task, but instead, whatever is of God is an assault on this sin-broken world: it is an invasion into the territory dominated by evil and ruled by Satan. Yet it is a *cosmos* which is suffering and causing distress, not as a rare occasion, but as a constant buzz in the warning system of pain, sometimes louder, sometimes softer, sometimes annoying, sometimes overwhelming, but always present:

> It grew harder and harder. Even within these four walls there was too much misery, too much seemingly pointless suffering. Every day something else failed to make sense, something else grew too heavy. "Will You carry this too, Lord Jesus?"
>
> But as the rest of the world grew stranger, one thing became increasingly clear. And that was the reason the two of us were here. Why others should suffer we were not shown. As for us, from morning until lights-out, whenever we were not in ranks for roll call, our Bible was the center of an ever-widening circle of help and hope. Like waifs clustered around a blazing fire, we gathered about it, holding out our hearts to his warmth and light. The blacker the night around us grew, the brighter and truer and more beautiful burned the word of God. "Who shall separate us from the love of Christ? Shall tribulation, or distress, or persecution, or famine, or nakedness, or peril, or sword? ... Nay in all these things we are more than conquerors through him that loved us."
>
> I would look about us as Betsie read, watching the light leap from face to face. More than conquerors. ... It was not a wish. It was a fact. We knew it, we experienced it minute by minute – poor, hated, hungry. We are more than conquerors. Not "we shall be." We are! Life in Ravensbruck took on two separate levels, mutually impossible: One, the observable, external life, grew every day more horrible. The other, the life we lived with God, grew daily better, truth upon truth, glory upon glory.   Corrie ten Boom[24]

On the shore of the Sea of Tiberius in John 21, the resurrected Jesus demonstrated His forgiveness and let Peter know of His continued confidence in him. He told Peter how he who had once been so cowardly would indeed give his life for his Lord. Peter catching sight of John, the beloved disciple, asks, "What about him?" Jesus answered, "If I will that he remain till I come, what is that to you? *You* follow Me" [v 22].

In answer to Maria, there is indeed a grand purpose which shows the suffering to be worthwhile. We have a hope to which to cling and watch as it comes closer and closer. We have a reward guaranteed in writing. We have a down payment "in hand," the Holy Spirit, so that we may be confident when all seems lost. We have proof that God is really on the ball and with us.

There is but one thing that remains:

Why are you here? "To obey Him," is Betsie's answer.

4. The Larger Picture

Blameless

One of the most famous examples of "innocent" suffering is, of course, Job. If only he knew that *God* initiates the conversation with Satan – baits the old crafty Serpent – in the first two chapters of his book, would his comment be a sarcastic, "Well, thanks a lot!!"? Perhaps. Or perhaps not.

As each of these two chapters opens, *God Himself* proclaims this man as blameless:

> Jehovah said to Satan, "Have you considered in your heart concerning My servant Job, that none is like him on the earth, a man blameless, upright, fearing God and turning from evil?" … [This statement is repeated] "who still firmly holds to his integrity, although you challenged Me to destroy him without cause." Job 1:8; 2:3

"Blameless" is used for John the Baptist's parents [Luke 1:6], and even by St Paul to describe his pre-conversion state [Philippians 3:6]. It does not mean perfect or holy – in Romans 1 through 3 Paul removes even the idea of "good enough" from the equation if we are trying to impress God enough to notice and to save us. However, "blameless" here indicates a man who is humbly and genuinely connected by faith and action to his God. Since this assessment of Job comes from Jehovah, we understand that what follows is not where a "bad" man has brought judgment upon himself. Since that is true, therefore his suffering must have a different reason.

John 9:2-3 reflects this idea, as the disciples ask Jesus the wonderfully philosophic question, "Rabbi, who sinned, this man or his parents, that he should be born blind?", but Jesus replies, "Neither this man sinned nor his parents, but that the works of God should be revealed in him." The "blind" man subsequently is shown to have clearer vision in regard to Who Jesus is than the "sighted" Jewish leaders. This understanding then sets the coming accusations of Job's "friends" into caricature, as they apply the same abstract philosophic approach to his suffering, as they accuse him and even his children of bringing the calamities upon themselves..

In response to Rabbi Kushner: Satan does not initiate anything in this dialogue – he only responds, and also must receive permission before he can act. This is clearly no contest between two equals, God and Satan, with God perhaps having the slight edge; instead Jehovah of Covenant is definitely in control, and therefore fulfilling a plan already established from before the world was created [reflected in Ephesians 1:4; 3:9; Colossians 1:26-27; II Timothy 1:9; Revelation 13:8]. Indeed "The Buck Stops Here" – Jehovah assumes final responsibility for all events as He says to Satan, "although you challenged Me to destroy him without cause," that is, although the Devil causes the tragedies, they occur by God's expressed consent: "Behold, all which he has is in your hand; but towards him you shall not lay a hand. ... Behold, he is in your hand, but preserve his life" [1:12; 2:6]. Although *Job* is "blameless," God takes the "blame" upon Himself.

This is reassuring because the time will never come where the Creator turns around and is startled by something which the Devil sneaks in – Satan's rebellion can only respond to that for which God first opens the door. However, it is also distressing, because both the good and the bad ultimately rests upon Jehovah's shoulders – He may not *do* the bad, nevertheless He *sees, allows and even initiates* the situation where the bad can happen.

"To Destroy Him Without Cause"

There are two competing desires in the contest we see in the opening chapters of Job. On the one hand is the Lord's desire to expose the surprising depth and tenacity of Job's faith; on the other hand, Satan's intent is that Job "will surely curse You to Your face!" [Job 1:11; 2:5].

When Creation was young, the Devil had jumped at the idea of rejecting God, and now, like an addict, rebellion fills the center of his vision, or as St Paul puts it: "All things are pure to the pure, but to the corrupt and incredulous nothing is pure" [Titus 1:15]. He thoroughly expects that anyone who is given the chance to reject Jehovah would not even think twice about the opportunity – in other words, such rebellion is inevitable. He believes that Job is merely acting "in his self-interest" since God is blessing him [Job 1:9-11; 2:4-5] – but take away the props …

Satan would seem to have the advantage here, since humanity by nature already leans so far toward rebellion that this man should literally be a pushover. Without God's props, the Devil should be able to puff softly in Job's direction and he would fall like a ton of bricks. What a triumph of defeat and exquisite suffering! Everything one thought he believed in, depended on, found comfort in, would be decimated. And the biggest fool, the betrayer who could not be escaped, would be one's own self. Everything has all been a self-delusion. There is nothing left but bleak despair with not even the attitude of "eat, drink, and be merry, for tomorrow we die" – just simply, "we die." Imagine: the physical suffering cannot hold a candle to this kind of spiritual suffering. Satan is in his glory.

This probably has worked for thousands, even for millions.

At the end of the book, the Devil likely would be seen walking away completely bewildered. The man wrestles, argues, confronts God, even curses his day of birth, yet despite every apparent logical reason, he does not do what Satan challenges through the mouth of his wife, "Do you still firmly hold to your integrity? Curse[25] God, and die" [Job 2:9]. Such faithfulness is just too foreign to the Devil's nature – after all, *his* whole being has already leapt at the chance to rebel against and to reject the Creator.

Preparing the Stage

Although rebellion is now part of the fabric of the universe, there is no random occurrence in the tragedies here, and, as Jesus declares in regard to the man born blind, such events need not be penalties for sins committed. No, our Lord states to His disciples that the affliction of the blind man is to reveal God's works. This is puzzling when the Creator on one hand describes His Glory in terms of goodness, grace, mercy, Steadfast Love, faithfulness, forgiveness and justice, and then declares that Job is a victim "without cause"

The book immediately sets out the premise that even "undeserved" suffering can be the platform upon which a greater task is accomplished. Job's initial chapters indicate that what is happening is not merely for Satan's sake; nor is it taking place in some obscure corner, as so often we think of our lives; nor is it the result of a "behind-closed-doors, in a smoky back room" deal between God and Satan; rather it is played out in the very throneroom of heaven, "when the sons of God came to present themselves before Jehovah" [Job 1:6; 2:1]. The stage through which God will reveal His glory is before all Creation – particularly angels, devils, us (and our neighbors) – and here the individual, Job, as with the blind man, has the lead role in the universe-wide drama. As Philip Yancey put it, "the view behind the curtain in chapters 1 and 2 reveals that Job was being exalted, not spurned. God was letting his own reputation ride on the response of a single human being."[26] Of such is often the role of suffering.

A prophecy was once given to a missionary couple at their commissioning, "You will have great suffering, and then you will have great joy." In India, after a number of fruitless years, as they drove to a worship service, their children were asking all sorts of questions about heaven. Then as they rounded a curve, another car crashed head-on with them. The three children did not survive. Alone in their hospital beds, the man and his wife remembered the prophecy and realized that God was acting within His Glory. They began to praise Him in the midst of their sorrow. After their recovery, they returned to their mission station and one of the first things they did was to hold a memorial service for their children. For most Indians, the death of a child is devastating. Many came because they wanted to know what this couple had that could give them the ability to celebrate the death of their children. And the prophecy indeed came true – they experienced great joy as many people became believers.

Betsy also understands, as she "drags" along a reluctant Corrie, that their suffering is not really the point, "without cause," but rather that it is the vehicle by which to touch so many lives with a genuine hope, that the overcrowding and even the fleas are merely tools by which the reality of their message could be spread. These are simply the tools by which the two women are positioned to significantly help where needed.

In one congregation of this writer, a woman in hospital was dying of a very painful cancer. Many times nurses, staff, even doctors would go out of their way to remark how in the midst of her agony, she was always patient and considerate, always grateful for their efforts. At her funeral, a large proportion of the congregation were from the hospital. Her suffering was "without cause," and yet others, perhaps as with Job even the whole *cosmos*, had observed her character.

Of course, the most classic example of innocent suffering is the Cross of Jesus. We cannot possibly understand the sorrow of the Father as He must stand by and watch His beloved only Son die, nor could we ever know the full weight of the suffering weighing upon that God/Man's shoulders. Again the universe is watching and Satan seems to be winning. Yet all is going according to a plan laid out long before, where something as unjust as the Cross is merely the platform upon which eternal life will be built. The *cosmos* witnesses as the drama of salvation reveals the intensity of God's Love.

Suffering is, well, *suffering* – anguish, agony, torment –, especially when it seems to be "without cause." Unfortunately our concept of "the world" is based on a type of tunnel vision in which we see only whatever is in our line of sight (not just physical sight); but the Creator's perspective encompasses a far greater view in *cosmic* proportions, in which the here-and-now is the meeting point of all the past and all the future. Still every so often we get a glimpse, a powerful demonstration, that we are not merely the pawns as we may sometimes think. Instead we hold crucial, pivotal roles for both humanity and universe, in which suffering provides the ideal stage where God ultimately reveals the awesome greatness of His Glory – especially of His Love – and also of the strength of our faith.

Worship??

In a single day, Job's wealth and livelihood, as well as his ten children[27] about whom he cares very deeply, are simply gone. In light of these enormous tragedies, what is his response?

> Job arose, tore his robe, shaved his head, then he fell to the ground and worshiped. He said: "Naked I came from my mother's womb, and naked shall I return there. Jehovah gave, and Jehovah has taken away; blessed be the Name of Jehovah." In all this Job did not sin nor foolishly condemn God. Job 1:20-22

"He fell to the ground and worshiped" – that is a bit of a shock! Even when afflicted by the painful boils, he simply says, "'Shall we accept good from God and not accept what is unpleasant?' In whole, Job did not sin with his lips" [Job 2:10]. How strange that his first response is to worship, even while wrestling with the apparent "without cause"! The book seemingly struggles with how one is to worship God while at the same time putting Him on trial, as Yancey observes:

> The remainder of the book [of Job] weaves together wonderful strains of dramatic irony, the most prominent being a double-hinged trial of integrity. To Job, God is on trial: How can a loving God treat him so unfairly? All of Job's legal briefs, however, are contained within the setting of the larger trial set up in chapters 1 and 2, the test of Job's faith. From our omniscient reader's viewpoint, we watch for cracks in Job's integrity as he loses, one by one, everything of meaning and value.
>
> It says something about our modern culture that we find such sympathy for Job's point of view. C. S. Lewis put his finger on the reason behind our empathetic response in his essay, "God in the Dock":
>
>> The ancient man approached God (or even the gods) as the accused person approaches his judge. For the modern man the roles are reversed. He is the judge: God is in the dock. He is quite a kindly judge: if God should have a reasonable defense for being the God who permits war, poverty and disease, he is ready to listen to it. The trial may even end in God's acquittal. But the important thing is that Man is on the Bench and God in the Dock.
>>
>> Philip Yancey[28]

Satan fully expects that Job in anguish will condemn Jehovah – "curse You to Your face!" What makes it even more likely is that Jehovah never tells this man why the ordeal is necessary – as CS Lewis puts it, "if God should have a reasonable defense ... The trial may even end in God's acquittal." But He never attempts to defend His actions to Job.

God's concluding message to this man is simply "Trust Me – I know you, you know Me, you know My Glory, and I know what I am doing." As strange as worship seems in the first chapter, its product is precisely to bring one to realize that very message: in worship we focus on the Lord – His wisdom, His power, His deeds, and especially the motivating force of His Steadfast Love as He really pays attention to individuals on this earth.

Worship draws us into the larger context of the Creator and of all Creation and of how eternity – ours as well as others – touches on a given experience. Even without all the details, we are reminded that the plan will draw to a worthwhile completion: "we know that for those who love God, He works all things together for good, for those who are called according to His revelation[29]" [Romans 8:28]. We have that confidence because we have seen the heart of God at work. Worship can be a powerful thing: it has the capacity to change our hearts and minds, to turn aside despair and point us toward hope.

Realistic?

Again Maria challenges in *The Hiding Place* film:

> And to the mindless, the words sound so comforting. In this place it is mockery.

Is worship truly a realistic response to such heartbreak, or is Job's reaction simply a contrived scenario as merely a literary tool to set the scene for the rest of the book? Do humans really have that capacity to worship in the midst of crushing tragedy? A more modern example might be found in the story behind the hymn "It is Well with My Soul":

> As a young man Horatio G Spafford had established a most successful legal practice in Chicago. Despite his financial success, he was described by George Stebbins, a noted Gospel musician, as a "man of unusual intelligence and refinement, deeply spiritual, and a devoted student of the Scriptures."
>
> Some months prior to the Chicago Fire of 1871, Spafford had invested heavily in real estate on the shore of Lake Michigan, and his holdings were wiped out by this disaster. Just before this he had experienced the death of his son. In 1873, he attempted to lift the spirits of his family by taking them on a vacation to Europe and also to assist Moody and Sankey in one of their Great Britain evangelistic campaigns. Due to unexpected last minute business, he had to remain in

Chicago; but sent his wife and daughters on ahead, planning to follow in a few days.

Off the Irish coast, the Villa du Havre was struck by the Lochearn and sank in twelve minutes. All four Spafford daughters drowned. Finally landing at Cardiff, Wales, Mrs. Spafford cabled her husband, "Saved alone."

Spafford left by ship to join his bereaved wife. As the ship passed about where his daughters had drown, with the verse, "He makes all things work together for good to them that love the Lord" (Rom 8:28) in mind, Spafford penned this hymn with words so significantly describing his own personal grief, "When sorrows like sea billows roll..." Yet Spafford focused attention in the third stanza on the redemptive work of Christ and in the fourth verse anticipated His glorious second coming. Able to overcome such personal tragedies and sorrows, Horatio Spafford could still say with such convincing clarity, "It is well with my soul."[30]

Another example is the history surrounding the hymn, "Now Thank We All Our God":

Martin Rinkart was called to pastor his native town of Eilenberg in 1617, just as Europe's 30 year religious war began. Famine and deadly diseases raged throughout the land. As a walled city, people from all around sought refuge in Eilenberg and overcrowding exaggerated the famine and pestilence. The Rinkart home served as a refuge for afflicted victims, even though it is said that Martin Rinkart often had difficulty in providing food and clothing for his own family.

The plague of 1637 was particularly severe. The superintendent left and two other clergymen died, Rinkart alone was left to minister to the city, sometimes preaching burial services for forty or more persons in one day. His wife died from the pestilence, and he himself fell ill, but survived. That year he buried 4480 people, indeed the population of Germany itself was reduced from 16 million to 6 million during these years. So when Rinkard wrote, "guide us when perplexed," truly he was not talking about minor inconveniences. Yet, he remained a faithful and caring pastor, tending to the sick and hungry.

Twice he dissuaded the Swedish army from imposing excessive tribute on these already impoverished people, yet he received little gratitude by the city authorities and was much harassed by them. He died exhausted on December 8, 1649. In the midst of suffering, death and rejection, looking to his Savior, he wrote sixty-six hymns, one in particular thanking God for the many blessings given to His People, the so-called "Te Deum of Germany": "Now Thank We All Our God."[31]

As described earlier, in Ravensbruck, Corrie watches the hope shining in the eyes of those gathered for worship and Bible study. Meanwhile half a world away, in a Japanese concentration camp, the same effects are being felt. In his book *Through the Valley of the Kwai*[32] (the true story of the bridge over the river; retitled as *To End All Wars*, with a movie also by that name), Ernest Gordon recounts how the prisoners move from an animalistic existence, to faith, to depth Bible study and to worship.

"The Dark Night of the Soul"

Job has the props knocked out from under him. What does he have now to sustain him as he wrestles not only with his loss but also with the silence of God? Gordon describes how easily when the prisoners initially face suffering, immediately they would turn to the props of religion to give them the easy way out:

> For most, religion was an attempt to find a quick and easy answer, a release from their fears. As human resources failed, men turned to God and said in effect,
> "Look, Old Boy, I'm in trouble. I'll speak well of you if you'll get me out of it."
> Churchgoing for many thus became a kind of insurance policy to protect them from personal suffering; religion a thing of formulas, ceremonials, and easy answers. They believed that if they cajoled God properly He could be persuaded to rescue them from the miseries of their present existence. They prayed for food, for freedom, or to be spared from death.
> The Bible they viewed as having magic properties; to the man who could find the right key, all would be revealed...
> The dominant motivation for such wholesale embracing of religion was not love and faith, but fear: fear of the unknown, fear of suffering, fear of the terror by night, fear of death itself, fear that made for division rather than for community.   Ernest Gordon[33]

However, like Job, they also experience the deafening silence of God. Faith is seen as useless – it makes no difference:

60

We had no church, no chaplains, no services. If there were men who kept faith alive in their hearts they gave no sign. This was not surprising. At Changi, many had turned to religion as a crutch. But the crutch had not supported them; so they had thrown it away. Many had prayed, but only for themselves. Nothing had happened. They had sought personal miracles from the Bible – and none had come. They had appealed to God as an expedient. But God apparently had refused to be treated as one.

We had long since resigned ourselves to being derelicts. We were the forsaken men – forsaken by our families, by our friends, by our government. Now even God had left us.

Hate, for some, was the only motivation for living. We hated the Japanese. We would willingly have torn them limb from limb, flesh from flesh, had they fallen into our hands. In time even hate died, giving way to numb, black despair.   Ernest Gordon [34]

CS Lewis, after the death of his wife, records his pain in the small book, *A Grief Observed*, and it identifies the bewilderment, loss, and emptiness which that pain encompasses. Although he did not expect to lose his faith, he still felt in chapter one:

But go to Him when your need is desperate, when all other help is vain, and what do you find? A door slammed in your face, and a sound of bolting and double bolting on the inside. After that, silence. You may as well turn away. The longer you wait, the more emphatic the silence will become. There are no lights in the windows. It might be an empty house. Was it ever inhabited? It seemed so once.   CS Lewis[35]

In this, Lewis and Job sound so similar. Yes, one can be confident of how God will indeed "make all things work together for good," but in the enormity of suffering, God seems to not want to touch them even with the proverbial "ten-foot pole." There is just a black hole where God should be.

The Jews would understand. In the four hundred years between the Testaments (Old and New), the cry is "Where is there a prophet among us?? God is silent!" – especially when the times are very bleak. A particularly dark period is during Antiochus IV – the self-proclaimed "Epiphanes"

("Illustrious One") or the Jews' nickname "Epimanes" ("Madman") —'s reign (about a hundred and seventy years before Jesus):

After being held for ransom in Rome for 13 years, Antiochus returns as an extreme Hellenist, eager to make the Jews "get on the Greek bandwagon." Jerusalem is renamed as "New Antioch"; the Scriptures, the Sabbath, the Circumcision, the sacrifices are forbidden. The highest bribe gets the High Priest office, and Antiochus controls the temple treasury. There is extreme cruelty toward those refusing to convert to the Hellenic "culture."

The Hasidim, "Pious Ones," are formed in reaction to such mockery of their religion, but Antiochus knows the Jews and their vulnerability. In response to their rebellion, he mounts a savage *Sabbath* attack, since the Jews would not "work" – fight – on the holy day. Jerusalem's walls are leveled. In the temple is *"The Abomination of Desolation / Appalling Sacrilege"* that Jesus' listeners might recall [Matthew 24:15; Mark 13:14]: in this holy place, Antiochus' troops hold orgies to Bacchus; a statue of Zeus Dionysius is installed; side rooms house cultic prostitutes for the Syrian soldiers; and swine are sacrificed on the altar, their blood sprinkled throughout the temple.

Meanwhile the Samaritans [which had been the northern ten tribes of Iarael] embrace Hellenization, disown their connection with the Jews, and rename their Mt Gerizim temple to honor Jupiter – this betrayal of their brothers in desperate need forms the backdrop to the animosity between the two groups during Jesus' time. Antiochus dies insane.

James Lindemann[36]

Where is God and why does He not come to rescue us? They are betrayed by their brothers, and God seemingly does not lift a finger, even when they give their lives to follow what His Law commands. The experience is only repeated in the Nazi holocaust.

Imagine what it is like for the disciples, to see their world, their hopes, even their faith literally collapse in on themselves as they watch their Lord, their beloved Master, the Messiah of their faith, die on the cross. Perhaps we do understand their anguish at not just merely a death, but the destruction of everything in which they believe, everything for which they hope, everything on which they depend. What more terrible pain can there be than such spiritual despair? As we also are left with shock and loss as we stand before the crosses of our lives – those times of confusion and even despair –, we also cannot see how anything worthwhile can come of such tragedy.

Of course, Jesus fully can identify with this feeling. Although an angel does come to strengthen Him in the Garden of Gethsemane, where is His Father when the real suffering takes place? Even the sun goes black. Even *He* cries out, "My God, My God, why have You forsaken Me?" [Matthew 27:46] – and He is *God's own Son*!

Yet we know that in the "dark night of the soul," in Jesus the Creator is saving His Creation; in those four hundred years of silence, the world and the Jews are being prepared for the Good News; CS Lewis gains a personal awareness of God's involvement in human life; Job is confronted with a vision of Jehovah's Creation-wide activity; and in the midst of atrocity and contempt a Savior will walk among and with the prisoners of war.

Faith Within Suffering

A light begins to shine in the Japanese death camps. Although "exhausted as men were by their work on the railroad, and subjected as they were daily to cruelties and deprivations in the camp,"[37] there are incidents of self-sacrifice, men stepping out to give of themselves, their time, their food, and even their lives for the sake of others. Some have been keeping the candle of faith burning even yet. The realization dawns that Jesus is no mere patch for when things are not comfortable, but rather He is the Guide, the ship's Pilot, Who comes aboard so that now He can lead them through the turbulent circumstances of which He personally understands. When all else has failed, now they become aware that Jesus has been truly standing among them all along:

Through our readings and our discussions we came to know Jesus. He was one of us. He would understand our problems because they were the sort of problems he had faced Himself. Like us, he often had no place to lay his head, no food for his belly, no friends in high places.

He, too, had known bone-weariness from too much toil, the suffering, rejection and disappointments that were part of the fabric of life. Yet he was not a killjoy. He would not have scorned the man who took a glass of wine with his friends or a mug of MacEwan's ale, or who smiled approvingly at a pretty girl. The friends He had were like our own and like us.

As we read and talked, he became flesh and blood. We saw him in the full dignity of manhood. He was a man we could understand and admire; the kind of friend we would like to have guarding our left flank; a leader we could follow.   Ernest Gordon[38]

It is a strange twist where a modern experience helps us understand a passage of the Bible instead of the reverse. The experience of the death camp, in which they discover not the yearned-for release from suffering but rather God's real presence in the midst of suffering helps us understand what was going on in the background for Job. In fact, it is in the suffering that they discover the concrete reality of the God-come-into-flesh, Jesus, rather than Someone Who is merely a religious figurehead. And as with Job, Jehovah does not explain himself to these men. The message to them is the same as to that man of old: "Trust Me!" or to Peter: "*You* follow Me."

When an acceptable answer was demanded of me, I had to go beyond Reason – I had to go to Faith. If I had learned to trust Jesus at all, I had to trust him here. Reason said, "We live to die." Jesus said, "I am the resurrection and the life."

In the light of our new understanding, the Crucifixion was seen as being of the utmost relevance to our situation. A God who remained indifferent to the plight of His creatures was not a God with whom we could agree. The Crucifixion, however, told us that God was in our midst, suffering with us.

We did not know the complete answer to the problem of suffering. But we could see that so much of it was caused by "man's inhumanity to man," by selfishness, by greed, and by all the forces of death that we readily support in the normal course of life. The cry of the innocent child, the agony I had seen in the eyes of a Chinese mother as she carried her dead baby, the suffering caused by earthquakes, fire, or floods, we could not explain. But we could see that God was not indifferent to such suffering.

We stopped complaining about our own. Faith would not save us from it, but it would take us through it. Suffering no longer locked us up in the prison house of self-pity but brought us into what Albert Schweitzer calls the "fellowship of those who bear the mark of pain,." We looked at the Cross and took strength from the knowledge that it gave us, the knowledge that God was in our midst.

Our lives were never free from the shadow of sadness. Our faith was tested daily by the suffering which we saw all around us, which we were now trying with our limited means and new-found truths to assuage.   Ernest Gordon[39]

The psychologist Abraham Maslow theorized that humans have a "hierarchy of needs" in which as the needs in one level are met, then the human is free to progress to the next level. So, once the "biological and physiological needs" are met, then one moves on to the "safety needs," then on to "belongingness and love needs," followed by "esteem needs," "cognitive needs," "aesthetic needs," "self-actualisation," and finally to "transcendence."

But in the concentration camps, where one is stripped of all of what are the usual props of life and of religion, Jesus simultaneously touches every level, from the top of the "hierarchy of needs" down.

Faith sustained us as individuals, but it also sustained the community of which we were a part. It shaped our culture, determined our morality, and gave unity to our common life. I would be absurd to say that faith and reason were separated; for faith led to reflection and reflection involved reason. Men who had very little education developed a keen interest in a variety of subjects ... Faith had inspired them to think creatively, to be aware of themselves, to be conscious of the ultimates, to be open to the world beyond their environment.   Ernest Gordon[40]

This journey through "the valley of the shadow of death" is often also experienced by those who face dying, whether their own death or of someone they love. They also travel through the panicked pleading, bargaining, and cajoling of God, only to sometimes be left with a bleak silence. Yet for many as they realize that the Lord is not going to "make it all go away," they are led to a more wonderful and greater understanding of what Jesus means when He says, "Lo, I am with you *always*." They are given not an escape, but rather new eyes and a new heart [Ezekiel 36:26; 44:7] to see the reality of the Creator hard at work within suffering to bring His Creation to Himself and to save it.

Equipped and Empowered

Therefore I make known to you that no one speaking in the Spirit of God says Jesus is accursed (or "Jesus be damned"), and no one can say "Jesus is Lord" if not in the Holy Spirit.   I Corinthians 12:3

Satan is looking for "the Big One" – not merely for the little rebellions which are rife in our daily lives (the battle between "the good that I would" and "the evil what I would not" [Romans 7:15-24]), but what he considers is the "inevitable" sin of utter rejection of God. He is counting on the assistance of our fallen human nature which already is aimed down that path. For him, the expectation is that of no real contest – Job will fall.

But as St Paul points out, the Holy Spirit is essential for any human to believe, no matter on which side of the Old/New Testament fence,[41] and St John comments in his first letter, "this is the victory that overcomes the world, our faith" [I, 5:4].[42] This cannot be unique to the New Testament, otherwise none of the Old Testament saints would have survived Satan's onslaughts. Poured out thousands of years later, still the Holy Spirit moves backwards through the Old Testament, working faith in Job, just as Jesus' death has effectiveness even for someone so far removed in the past as Adam and Eve. The Pentecost event is not robbed of its extraordinary nature, but rather filled with an awesome awareness of how He truly and literally is "poured out upon all flesh" [Acts 2:17; Joel 2:28] – upon the *totality* of human existence.

So as the book opens, Job is already a believer in a very personal relationship with Jehovah; therefore in his Holy Spirit-incited faith he is equipped to not succumb to the enormous suffering from Satan's very forceful temptation. Even when Jehovah does not "seem" to be very nice, much to Satan's shock, Job's expected sin is not inevitable at all – he can and does choose not to "curse God and die." This man indeed is equipped to "overcome the world" by his faith – he overcomes natural and manmade disasters, he overcomes the attempted erosion of faith by his "comforters," he overcomes Satan's attempt to spiritually destroy him "without cause."

The Redeemer

And here begins worship. In the Japanese labor camps, it is not in cozy security and based upon the props of a comfortable life, but rather by men reduced to skeletons by malnourishment, hard work, and disease, daily surrounded by others dying[43] and by the extreme cruelty of their captors. It is the kind of worship that the Ravensbruck inmates would understand. It is the kind of worship Job, Spafford, Rinkard would understand.

This is no feeble resignation of a hopeless victim to what can seem to be a capricious God, but rather as a confident assurance of a person who knows with Whom he is dealing. In Chapter 19, on one hand Job describes his feelings in that his three "friends" persecute him as God does [v 22], and yet he responds to his very own statement by declaring:

> Oh that my words were now written; oh that they were inscribed in a book and were engraved with an iron pen and lead in rock forever! For I know that my Redeemer lives, and in the end He shall arise over the dust; and after my skin is destroyed, yet in my flesh I shall see none other than God (Whom I shall see for myself and my eyes shall behold). How my heart yearns within me!   vv 23-27

Yes, the edge of suffering is very real and terribly sharp – and yet it is also blunted by how the picture is far greater than just these particular moments. Despite being "without cause" in his suffering, Job (and the other sufferers) factors in a resurrection and an eternity, and he expects this seemingly puzzling God to be his Redeemer.

The Hebrew word for "Redeemer" is interesting: it is used for the special "family office" of what might be called the "Blood balancer," the *Go'el.* This is the person who redeems a family member who has been sold into slavery and is the "avenger" when life is taken from the family [Numbers 35:12-27; Deuteronomy 19:1-12; Joshua 20:1-9]. It is the word of choice when God declares He will "redeem" Israel from the slavery of Egypt [Exodus 6:6; 15:13]. In the Book of Ruth, Boaz holds the office and his task is to see that the Bloodline of Elimelech is restored [Ruth 3:9, 12-13; 4:1-8]; and the baby who now reestablishes the Bloodline is himself called a *Go'el* [4:14]. Of course, the Psalms use the word especially in regard to the Lord [for example, 69:18; 74:2; 103:4; 106:10]. The *Go'el's* mission is not so much focused on retribution but rather to return life and the family back into balance.

Job therefore indicates that there will come a day in which all shall be brought back into balance: the loss of life, the suffering, the grief, and especially his own life – *he* will be redeemed so that he for himself shall see God; and will also be avenged against the one who has brought such suffering and loss of life to his family.

Uh … but Jehovah establishes that He is the One Who is ultimately responsible! Will the Creator call *His own Self* to account?

As a contemporary to Abraham, is Job given an insight into the "mystery hidden for ages," the awareness which Abraham perhaps realizes [Genesis 22:1-19], where the Redeemer will ultimately be God's own only Son as the Lamb of sacrifice? Does he recognize that Jehovah, although not actually doing the tragedy (and Satan will ultimately be punished), still in the end will avenge the loss of life upon Himself to bring all life back into balance?

Hebrews 6:13 declares, "For God, having made a promise to Abraham, because He could swear by no one greater, He swore on His own Self" – in other words, the Lord makes Himself both Participant and Overseer of His Covenant relationship. He will hold Himself accountable for His promises and relationship to humans, even to where it ultimately costs Him His own Life. With humans, being both participant and overseer does not work very well, but God demonstrates that He will not back down from either role.

We have no idea about what Job has at his fingertips concerning God's activity and messianic promises, therefore we must be careful about ascribing too much ignorance to him. This ancient man seems to have a good awareness of Jehovah's ultimate plan even though he struggles (as even we "New Testament" folk also often do) with the meaning of what is happening now "without cause." In this confidence of knowing his God and knowing some of what this God is ultimately about in the light of eternity, he worships.

This hymn had the sound of victory. To me it said,

"Man need never be so defeated that he can do nothing. Weak, sick, broken in body, far from home, and alone in a strange land, he can sing! He can worship!"   Ernest Gordon [44]

Health, Wealth, Happiness and Hope

Some groups seem to emphasize that if we are not "healthy, wealthy and happy," then there is something direly wrong with our faith and lives, because if we did what God wanted, we would have no problems. The message is similar to Job's "comforter" Eliphaz' perspective:

Remember, pray thee: who was innocent who ever perished? where were the righteous ever destroyed?

Those who I have seen plow iniquity and sow trouble harvest it.

From the breath of God they perish, and by the blast of his anger they are consumed. ...

In six troubles He will deliver you, yes, in seven evil shall not touch you.

In famine He will redeem you from death, and in war from the power of the sword.

From the scourge of the tongue you will be hidden, and you will not be afraid of violence when it comes.

At destruction and famine you will laugh, and of the beasts of the earth you will not fear.

For with the stones of the field you will have a Covenant, and the beasts of the field will be at peace with you.

You will know that peace is in your tent; you will attend to your home and no sin [will be there].

You will know that your descendants will be many, and your offspring as the grass of the earth.

You shall come in full strength to the grave, as when the mature grain is bundled (stooked). ` Job 4:7-9; 5:19-25

But what we find is that even though one can thank God as Betsy does for the fleas, and praise God in worship as do Gordon, his fellow prisoners and the others, still none are taken out of their situations The fleas do not disappear or refuse to bite Betsy and her sister, the prisoners still have cruelty and death surrounding them while their bodies waste away, Spafford and Rinkard are not released from the grief of their losses.

They rather discover the maturity of a relationship with their Lord Who is not afraid of using even suffering to bring His salvation into this world, as St Paul would affirm:

in every way hard oppressed, yet not crushed; perplexed, but not despairing; persecuted, but not forsaken; cast down, but not annihilated – always carrying in the body the death of Jesus, that also the Life of Jesus might be clearly visible in our body. For unceasingly we who live are handed over to death for Jesus' sake, so that the Life of Jesus also might be clearly visible in our mortal flesh; so then death works in us, but Life in you. II Corinthians 4:8-12

70

The seemingly odd result of experiencing such suffering and being confronted with crushing adversity – not just physical but also spiritual – can be that the end product is not despair but, of all things, *hope*:

> Therefore, having been justified by faith, we have peace with God through our Lord Jesus Christ, through Whom also we have access by faith into this grace in which we stand, and we boast in *hope* of the Glory of God [consider how that Glory is defined in Exodus 33 and 34: grace, mercy, goodness, Covenant, Steadfast Love, faithfulness, forgiveness and justice!].
>
> Not only that, but we also boast in tribulations, knowing that tribulation produces steadfastness; and steadfastness, tested character; and tested character, *hope*. The hope does not humiliate us, because God's Love has been poured into our hearts through the Holy Spirit Who has been given to us.   Romans 5:1-5

This both Corrie and Gordon witnessed amid the death and suffering in the concentration camps: *hope* really can be formed in the midst of suffering, because even there the Love of God can be discovered, poured out through the profound working of the Holy Spirit..

And at the end of the book of Job, Satan walks away, shaking his head in bewilderment.

5. Expanding Ripples

The Bridge over San Luis Rey

Thorton Wilder's novel begins by describing the collapse of an ancient bridge while five people are on it. A monk, who himself is about to enter the bridge, witnesses the event and wonders why did particularly these people die in this chance occurrence. He sets out to discover all he can about their lives and about God's plan for each. What he discovers is that each life does not have a straight line to the bridge collapse, but rather that each weaves its way throughout other lives and circumstances. Then at the tragedy it is like when a voice suddenly gives out half-way through a sentence and leaves the listener (or at least, *this* reader) frustrated by what is still unresolved as each person's future suddenly ceases. Unfortunately, that is often the case in the non-fiction (real) world.

The novel identifies that the bridge collapse is not merely one "lump sum" tragedy, merely a pebble dropped into a pond, but rather as the ripples expand outward, each of the five people is a unique life interconnected with other lives. As we also observe various calamities, it is necessary for us as well to not only see the individuals on whom we focus, as important as they are in their own right, but also to realize how they are so entwined with others that the suffering often casts a wider net than just solitary persons.

Complexity

With Job, we are privileged to see what Wilder's monk could only guess at: besides the visible earthly side, we glimpse a heavenly, universe-wide aspect in parallel to his suffering, of which neither he nor his human observers are aware.

73

Also often when we consider Job, we forget that this particular incident, is just *one* relatively small slice of his life. Does he live "happily ever after"? Really? As a human in this world, that is highly unlikely. Even in the temptations of Jesus, when Satan is finished, Luke records, "he departed from Him *until an opportune time*" [4:13]. Yes, Satan has played his big hand and has lost, but by no means does he consider himself out of the game. Imagine what it must be like for Job and his wife whenever any of his subsequent children gets sick.

What about his original ten children who die? After all, they are not incidentals! In Wilder's novel, the five whom we would usually barely notice, the monk seeks out their personal stories – but who takes that role in investigating what God has been doing with each of Job's children? Are they merely expendable "filler" to the Job account? But they are significant! They have their place within God's unfolding of His design, just the same as "unimportant" each of us also has our place in that great plan.

What about others who also suffer in the midst of this tragedy? What is Jehovah doing among the servants and their families, friends and others? They are not *our* concern – or else the book would become way too large – but they certainly are *His*. Not only on earth, what is going on in heaven on *their* behalf? After all, it is not as if the universe pauses while we focus on Job alone, nor is the struggle only for the more famous or more wealthy. The Lord often emphasizes His concern for the powerless and helpless, the widows and orphans and the like, which means that those who are insignificant to us – nameless ones in someone else's story – are yet very valuable to Him and to His Plan. Just like with the five on Wilder's *Bridge*, each individual has surprising importance:

Why does God permit, even encourage, such tests of faith? Could it possibly matter to God whether one man or one woman accepts or rejects him? Elihu, the last and most mysterious of Job's comforters, voiced such a question scornfully to Job:

If you sin, how does that affect him?
If your sins are many, what does that do to him?
If you are righteous, what do you give to him, or what does he receive from your hand?
Your wickedness affects only a man like yourself, and your righteousness only the sons of men. (Job 35:6-8, NIV)

The opening chapters of Job, however, reveal that God had much at stake in one man's wickedness or righteousness. Somehow, in a way the book only hints at and does not explain, one person's faith made a difference. A tiny piece of the history of the universe was at stake.

Philip Yancey[45]

Therefore, how much does Job represent *thousands* of other "Jobs," who, although never having a book written about them, yet have been just as crucial in the drama of heaven and earth? In an additionally mysterious sense, St Paul informs us that this is not merely a lump sum total of isolated individuals but that an often unrealized yet essential element is the corporate involvement of believers as Christ's unified Body, in its "Image of God" to Creation and to "the sons of God [angels]" [Job 1:6]:

that *through the Church* the manifold wisdom of God might now be made known to the principalities and powers in the heavenly places.

Ephesians 3:10

Job's Wife

A pastor and his wife are going through a very hurtful time. As he is attempting to find comfort for the both of them in the promise in which God would make all things work together for good, his wife erupts, "No, He won't!" Not offended, the pastor is surprised at the vehemence, suddenly realizing in just how great a degree his wife has been suffering in this circumstance. It is then when he begins to have a whole new respect for Job's spouse.

Job's wife is suffering, crying out in the agony of losing *her* children. Many people criticize her as if she ought to be insensitive to her loss and therefore should be a pillar of strength for Job. Yet grief is real and often is accompanied by anger and other visceral feelings. It is a rage against death, but since death is an intangible, the target gets shifted to something more defined: at perhaps the spouse, or at the dead, or at any survivors, and frequently at God. The death of a child creates a terrible loneliness – as one bereaved parent remarked, "Who do you lean on when the one you depend on is already doubled over with their own grief?" A sad reality is that many grieving couples are divorced within one year of their child's death. And in Job's and his wife's loss, this is *ten – all* their children – suddenly dead.

Job's wife has the additional agony and isolation as she watches her husband suffer – an agony accented by the frustration of being helpless. He, at least, is occupied by the battle, but for her, there is only endless "useless" waiting, which most humans do not handle well. Is being shut out as a mere bystander not sometimes the hardest and most exquisite of torments?

How many have wished to hasten such an equally unbearable and truly heart-wrenching situation to its end? How easily the wild desperation for the suffering to stop can cause something similar to "Curse God and die!" to cross the mind! Yes, her outburst is wrong, imprudent at best, and yet it does not necessarily mean rejection of the Lord – nor rejection by the Lord. One thinks of the death camp prisoners, who abandoned the initial "easy" faith, only to later return to a faith of a greater maturity – and to discover the evidence of God's acceptance and reaffirmation of such "prodigal sons."

Is Job the only one who matters, or is God simultaneously doing something in his wife's life? Although she does not have a book on *her* suffering, would the universe also be observing her as well?

The Perpetrator

And, as Betsy pointed out on an earlier page, in the wider ripples of suffering, what about the person responsible for evil, for example, the person who had betrayed them to the Gestapo (Jan Vogel) – *he* is suffering. perhaps in self-guilt, broken relationships (for example, ostracized by his fellow townspeople) and such; or perhaps sensitivity to pain's warning has been destroyed and he *suffers* in the dangerous ignorance of spiritual leprosy. Is his Creator not also caring about him? After all, St Paul declares that even while we were all of us "still sinners … enemies, we were reconciled to God through the death of His Son" [Romans 8:8, 10]. How like Corrie, we concentrate on the innocent victim and often are content to dismiss (or worse) the perpetrator, yet did Jesus not die for the sins of the *whole* world [I John 5:2] – for the one who inflicts suffering as well? We want that person to be punished, but as Corrie realized, he also has been invited into the forgiveness and life of the Cross.

There is confusion here that needs to be addressed even if it is not directly related to our main topic: ought we pray for such "vessels of wrath bound for destruction"? And for what do we pray?

For He says to Moses, "I will have mercy on whom I have mercy, and I will have compassion on whom I have compassion." So therefore, it depends not on him who wills, nor on him who strives, but on Him Who shows mercy – God!
For the Scripture says to Pharaoh, "for this very reason I therefore lifted you out, so that I might show in you My power, so that My Name should be declared in all the earth." Therefore, then, to whomever He wills He shows mercy, and to whomever He wills He hardens.
You then will say to me, "Why does He still find fault? For who has resisted His will?" Really, o man? Who are you to dispute with God? Shall the thing molded say to its maker, "Why have you made me thus?"
Does not the potter have authority over the clay, out of the same lump to make one vessel for honor and another for disgrace? What if God's desire is to show wrath and to make known His power, has borne

with much patience the vessels of wrath destined for destruction, that He might make known the riches of His Glory upon the vessels of mercy, which He prepared beforehand for Glory, whom He has also called, even us – not only from the Jews but also from the Gentiles?

Romans 9:15-24

In II Timothy 2:20, St Paul adds: "…are there only vessels of gold and silver but not also of wood and earthenware, and some for honor and some for disgrace?"; St Peter writes "…who stumble at the Word, being rebellious for which they were also appointed" [I, 2:8; as well as Jude 1:4 and Proverbs 16:4]). However, the tension is that Jesus died, *in Love*, for *"the whole world"* [I John 2:2; John 3:16], Peter also says, "The Lord … is patient toward you, not willing for any to perish but that all come to repentance" [II, 3:9], while Paul adds, "…not realizing that God's kindness is to lead you to repentance?" [Romans 2:4]; and in an earlier letter to Timothy:

This is good and acceptable before God our Savior, Who desires all men to be saved and to come to the knowledge of the truth.

I Timothy 2:3-4

Does "the whole world" or "all men" only mean those who are approved, while the rest are to be discarded? Humans play those games with words, but does God stoop to such convenient doubletalk and apparent dishonest meanings? In dealing with the Creator's foreknowledge in the time-bound progression of daily life, humans are confused: is "knowing the end from the beginning" [Isaiah 46:10] creative or predictive? Does it *cause* something to be, or simply *predict* it will be – or, in a mystery we cannot understand, both?

When God says that He will harden Pharaoh's heart, is He saying that Pharaoh has no choice; or is it that this king is "so dyed in the wool" committed to rebellion the he will allow himself no other option – that no matter what God does, he simply will end up with a harder heart? Still, either way Jehovah has no problem "tweaking the nose" of this king, and truly this Pharaoh will ultimately be used to demonstrate God's power and Glory as the story is retold the world over throughout coming generations.

Often we look at the really big offenders in regard to causing suffering, but does not the leveling of God's Law also accuse us of doing the very same things we decry? We criticize a fellow driver of doing "something really stupid" or "just inconsiderate" and then, literally within a week or so, we do the same action? How often do we defend ourselves that in our case it is necessary or forgivable? How often is the person condemned because of our other-than-righteous motivations? This is Corrie's point in the earlier quote, when she realizes that the attitude which drives Jan Vogel also resides in her own heart, even if it is not as visibly evident.

Is "the vessel for disgrace" an eternal condemnation, or is it simply a station in life which reveals spiritual destitution, yet God still does call people out from that state into His salvation and some do respond? Are there not examples of, for example, ex-mafia "enforcers," ex-biker gang members, ex-Gestapo officers (as Corrie faced), and others who have turned away from the "disgraceful" vessel and have been transformed into the earthen vessels which hold the Glory of God [II Corinthians 4:7]?

Yes, Jehovah in His foreknowledge identifies who will finally be saved, but the how and the results of such precognition are not within our understanding. It will always be a mystery to us in how He can "design" "vessels for wrath" while at the same time sincerely and lovingly call all to repentance, "not wishing that any should perish." Actually, this does have something to say to our subject, as we contemplate whether anyone is merely "cannon fodder" in the contest between God and evil, merely incidental "filler" in a person's story, or whether even *their* lives are *significant* to the heart of God and to the death of Jesus.

The Holy Innocents

This then is a good place to return to the Holy Innocents who die by Herod's hand while the Holy Family is enroute to Egypt. In a sense they are in a similar position as Job's ten children – although they play a major role in their own personal dramas (of which we do not know), we see them as *simultaneously also* having a role in other people's dramas (their family's and particularly Jesus').

We cannot help it, but we often measure value by the list of accomplishments a person has done, so when we look at an infant, we are appalled when they have had no opportunity to compile such a list – all they have is unfulfilled potential. Or do they? What constitutes a "wasted life" or "unfilled potential" in eternity?

With the Creator, the understanding is different – age is immaterial to Him: one does not have to be above twenty years old to begin his tasks. In fact, we have seen young children, even severely handicapped children, who by their demonstration of simple yet determined faith and love put seasoned adults to shame, which calls us to re-evaluate the standards by which we evaluate people, the world – and even God. Indeed, does Jesus not tell us to have the faith of "a little child" [Matthew 18:2-5; 19:13-14] – and this without the expected noble "accomplishments"?

Given to such innocents might be the necessary role (among the rest) to call into the open what is inside another human being, without which the inner quality could never be exposed: as in Job's case, the suffering which reveals that in spite of his bewilderment he maintains a confidence in His Lord; and as with Herod, the utter rejection of God and cruelty to which human sin can too easily and quickly degenerate. In the great clash between God and evil: Jobs, Herods and the innocent are essential to understand all

80

that is at stake in this conflict – this is no casual faith, nor casual evil, nor casual suffering which are involved!

Again, it is important to reflect on the reason for why humans exist at all: "the Image of God" – we are to be the way by which the universe glimpses Him. The point here is not to argue whether a child is old or young, innocent and pure or not, and so forth, but rather to indicate that when Jehovah is satisfied with the task as given to a certain individual, why should He not have the right to say, "You have accomplished that which I set before you" – and for those who hold to Him, "You have been faithful over a little, I will set you over much" [Matthew 25:21, 23]? What more *can* a person do, and what more can a person humble before his Creator *want* to do?

What is unfortunate is that this explanation can be very detached, while the situation is very emotional. And yet if there is to be real comfort, it must be grounded in something which is solid, which then can help give stability to the emotions. Unlike the monk, who attempted to look into the life of each person to see what (he thought) God was carrying out in the midst of tragedy; but rather more like Job who could only pursue an unanswered "Why??", we most often can only echo Corrie's words, "… one thing became increasingly clear. And that was the reason the two of us were here. Why others should suffer we were not shown."[46] Gordon had written, "The cry of the innocent child, the agony I had seen in the eyes of a Chinese mother as she carried her dead baby, the suffering caused by earthquakes, fire, or floods, we could not explain. But we could see that God was not indifferent to such suffering."[47]

God accomplishes a unique task in regard to each of the Holy Innocents, and to each of their families, and to us – they are not merely part of an incidental lump sum.

"There is a Season, and a Time ..."

There is an appointed time to everything - a time to every purpose under the heaven:
A time to give birth, and a time to die;
A time to plant, and a time to uproot what is planted;
A time to kill, and a time to heal;
A time to smash in pieces, and a time to build up;
A time to weep, and a time to laugh;
A time to mourn, and a time to dance;
A time to throw stones, and a time to gather stones;
A time to embrace, and a time to shun embracing;
A time to find, and a time to lose;
A time to preserve, and a time to fling away;
A time to tear, and a time to sew;
A time to be still, and a time to speak;
A time to love, and a time to hate;
A time to battle, and a time to be at peace.   Ecclesiastes 3:1-8

How does one decipher the ebb and flow of life: why does this happen *now* and not later? why does it happen *here* and not there? why does the negative have to be part of each couplet in the passage? Dr Brand indicated that, at least in this fallen world, there must be a necessary balance between suffering and pleasure in order to give meaning to both – that although we may not appreciate the dark, in a tapestry there is value to the contrast between it and light. There is value in even the undesirable experiences: St Paul declares them to be an equipping:

Blessed be the God and Father of our Lord Jesus Christ, the Father of compassion and God of all comfort, Who comforts us in all our affliction, so that we may be able to comfort those who are in any affliction through the comfort with which we ourselves are comforted by God. Because as Christ's sufferings abound in us, so through Christ our comfort also abounds. If we are afflicted, it is for your comfort and salvation; and if we are so comforted, it is for your comfort, working steadfastness in the same sufferings which we suffer.
                                                        II Corinthians 1:3-6

He links the comfort in suffering with steadfastness, and truly there is the aspect of a steadfastness which comes from humbly allowing Jehovah to be the God of life, the God of our whole – and day-to-day – life. It is the steadfastness of Corrie, Gordon and their fellow prisoners who discover the strange comfort of a Creator Who does not necessarily remove them from suffering but equips them to experience His presence and the steadfastness of His Love. It is a powerful comfort because they are equipped to enter into the suffering of others, not with glib and empty reassurances, but rather with a concrete hope to which suffering must yield.

The comfort of which St Paul speaks is remarkable – it is ongoing in its effects: it is not only of value in the given situation, but also again and again it will surface as one encounters others who have need of it. Possibly it may happen where the experience of suffering is separated by years to when the comfort is used to strengthen someone else. The suffering may seem to be an isolated mystery, yet it becomes an important connection to another person now at this time. How often does the suffering of innocents trigger a movement which calls others to become involved, which may only bear important fruit after a period of time, such as the international child help organizations which rose in response to starvation and other needs in nature-, poverty- and war-ravaged areas of the world.

Not only does the suffering expand in ever larger circles to touch and influence other people's lives, but one might also see the inverse in which in ever expanding circles others are called to minister to the original individual's suffering, as Paul later continues:

> Also your helping jointly by prayer for us, to the end that many people will give thanks concerning us for the gift given on account of the many prayers. II Corinthians 1:11

The net of suffering often is thrown wider than we realize, including both those in an immediate circle around the sufferer, as well as those in future settings.

Too Much to Handle

This chapter identifies that there is a great deal of complexity as we consider the larger involvement of people, suffering and purpose beyond the "noticed" individuals (like Job). We should not be faulted for normally not thinking about these others, otherwise the volume of information rapidly becomes too enormous for us to handle. So, for example, we can only concentrate on Job, because this is enough of a task. To be able to handle the whole larger circle of any suffering really requires a mind of the Creator's capacity. He does account for each and every one, because He cares about them as well – just the same as He cares about each of us, even down to "the hairs of your head" [Matthew 10:30]. When we realize that eternity must also be factored into the equation, how foolish and inadequate is our grasp of all which any given situation contains.

Every once in a while, though, we do discover how a person who appeared to be a "bit player" in someone else's drama also has his own script for his life. We become aware of the interweaving of people within a much larger tapestry in which God keeps track of every thread, each with its own specific outcome, even of those of whom *we* are not mindful or even of whom we choose to ignore. Yet if we were to follow any one of the threads: it crosses *many* others, sometimes above, sometimes below, sometimes in front, sometimes in back. Perhaps another thread comes to help fill in the color, or enhance it, or contrast it – or is it the other way around? or both? –; some may run alongside for a distance, others are so short it seems to be only a dot; some disappear only to reappear farther down the line.

How can we know the full picture? There is no "one size fits all" – as if one story encompasses all sufferers. We just are not privy to the range of elements involved, and so we are left dissatisfied with an unanswerable question "Why?" God is handling each case of suffering, no matter upon which one we may focus, accomplishing what He sees is necessary in each case within its wider application. How can we demand of God a single, simple explanation for any given experience, since far more is involved: the cause, purpose and resolution of *each* event, of each life, is tailored to that individual within the combined effects (both seen and unseen) of perhaps hundreds of "threads" involved, within a time span of perhaps generations?

Yet when the work has been completed, the Weaver guarantees that every thread will be exactly in its right place, and the picture – the Image as He has determined – will be exactly the way it should be.

Oral Roberts once told of the night when he received word that his daughter and her husband had died in a plane crash.[48] As he and his wife drove to tell their young grandchildren that their parents were not coming home again, as they wrestled with what they would say, a message came to his mind to comfort him, "God knows something about this that you do not know." That simple message was picked up by others and became a source of comfort for many, reminding them that the Weaver was still working, "making all things work together for good" [Romans 8:28], as He promised.

God, I Want to Talk to You About Your Judgments!

Righteous are You, O Jehovah, however I would contend with You: I would discuss with You Your judgments: Why does the way of the wicked prosper? Why are those happy who deal in treachery?

Jeremiah 12:1

However, it is a relief that Jeremiah says what he does – we are not alone in our reaction to the suffering around us, because like him neither are we really very happy with the explanation so far given, nor should we be content with how evil destroys our world and our lives. So it really is nice to hear a *prophet* – and a major one at that – with hand on hip, waggle his finger at the Lord in bewilderment! He basically says,

> Jehovah, God of Covenant, You of course are righteous, but as I look at Your judgments, I really want to talk to You about them!! Why do the wicked seem to get away with their wickedness? Why do the faithless deceivers seem so happy?

Thank you, Jeremiah, for bluntly expressing what fairly often is in the back of *our* minds! You are not lounging on a comfortable "authority chair": you struggle; you just want to give up; and you are so disheartened at what happens all around you! Your People for whom you care so deeply, blithely go from bad to worse, ignoring the irritating warning that something is dreadfully wrong and that the Lord is about to withdraw His call to repentance! You cry out for the innocent victims of callous evil: the fatherless and widows, the innocent children and the helpless families – it is not just the seeming abandonment of God, but how that rebellion is becoming ever more entrenched into daily life. You are only the messenger, and yet you are beaten and disgraced [for example, 20:2; 38:6]. Talk about suffering: you complain that your task is just too painful in which to continue, and yet too painful to stop:

> I say, "I will not make mention Him, nor speak anymore in His Name" – but in my heart it becomes like a burning fire shut up in my bones; I am weary of holding it in, and I cannot.   Jeremiah 20:9

As Jeremiah suffers both internally and externally, he seems to walk that thin line between faith and non-faith – the same line on which we also sometimes precariously balance. Yet, just like him, we also find that we cannot simply let go of our faith –His word "in my heart becomes like a burning fire" – , and – just like him – we can feel that we are on a spit being roasted over that "burning fire."

Is it wrong to challenge God? No. God will not sail out of heaven in arrogance to squash us. The manger in Bethlehem proved that although He had ample right to do that, instead He comes to restore us. The Cross defines how deeply and powerfully He is determined to rid His Creation of evil. Yet in the midst of our bewilderment, although we cannot fathom why there is suffering in regard to others, as Corrie and Betsy realized, *our* main task is how *we* will act as representatives of His Image:

> He has declared to you, O man, what is good; and what does Jehovah seek from you but to do justly, to love Steadfast Love [HESED], and to humbly walk with your God! Micah 6:8

He does expect that we in turn obediently and humbly listen to Him, realizing that due to the limits of our understanding, in the midst of all this, He simply calls for us to have faith and to be His light into this world.

Not Immune

Since God has allowed the choice to "not love," He reasonably must also allow the consequences of the choice, which means that there will always be innocent victims young and old. Only in this way will evil's real nature be exposed before the universe, for all can now see for themselves what evil costs, and come face-to-face with the horror, whether it be in the Nazi and Japanese death camps, in "the killing fields" of Pol Pot, or in the abuse of a child. Jehovah "turns up the pain" in order to confront humanity with the realization that there is something drastically wrong, fatally wrong in our world.

But this is not some abstract, dispassionate exercise! When Jesus sets foot on the earth, we are aware of a timeless personal involvement which the Creator Himself has with suffering, as the God of eternity meets the agony and abandonment of the Cross, taking upon Himself in the past, Job's and his wife's loss and grief, and their children's experience with death itself; while also experiencing the destitution and despair of the death camps, and the horror of the abuse in our own society.

God the Father, of course, has never detailed what it was like for Him to watch His own, only-begotten, well-beloved Son die. Yet imagine for the moment: the all-powerful Creator Whose very Word brings Creation out of nothing – not out of *virtually* nothing, but *really out of nothing* –, to Whom nothing is impossible. Worlds, universes are at His fingertips, and yet *His Son* is on the Cross suffering. *His Son* is crying out to Him. *His Son is dying!* One could easily imagine a path worn in heaven, paced in the agony of the God of the universe Who can only watch, helpless to do anything, unable to lift a finger – it is Job's wife's helplessness in eternal proportions.

What is it which has so tied the hands of this ultra-powerful Father? The answer simply is Love – but how so? Is not the Son the Father's most beloved Object in the universe? What could make the Father so tie down *this* Love so as to make Him unable to alleviate any of that suffering? The bewildering answer is: His Love *for us.* But how can this be? He simply cannot love us more than His own Son! Yet this is *His, and His Son's,* choice! Here is the full size to the tapestry, here is the awareness of how there is so much more to the picture than a single thread, yet one single Thread does hold the tapestry together and It enriches the brilliance to be found in the ordinary threads which make up the complete Image.

Although suffering is distasteful to us, and although the Lord fully understands its cost and effect, He is not afraid of it and will use it as necessary to bring to completion His Image in a universe infected by evil, as He reveals not just evil's destruction of life, but also demonstrates His blessings through which He moves us closer to eternal life by His side.

As Corrie and Betsy, and the prisoners in the Japanese death camp discovered, they would not be removed from the suffering, but neither will Jehovah remove Himself from the suffering. He will walk together with them – and us – *within* the suffering and in that experience He will touch the lives of many more, even to generations in the future. With everyone, He will weep over grief, wrestle with frustration, deal with discouragement, experience betrayal. He will know cruelty and be condemned for no just cause. He will know agony and great pain, and yet although He Himself was, He will not abandon *us*.

Indeed the net of suffering has been cast *very* wide.

6. The Breadth of Repentance

Repent!

The Plea and Warning to Repent

> Some were present at that time telling Him about the Galileans whose blood Pilate had mingled with their sacrifices. Jesus answered them, "Do you think that these Galileans were sinners beyond all other Galileans, because they suffered such things? I tell you, no; but unless you repent you all will likewise perish.
>
> Or those eighteen on whom the tower in Siloam fell and killed them, do you think they were debtors beyond all other men who dwelt in Jerusalem? I tell you, no; but unless you repent you all will in like manner perish.   Luke 13:1- 5

It is as obvious as Genesis 3 that much suffering comes on the account of our sins. Adam and Eve sin and bring evil into the world, resulting in suffering coming upon them and consequently upon their descendants. Israel and Judah have unabashedly forsaken their Covenant Partner, Jehovah, and are sent off into captivity. An "indiscretion" infects a woman with syphilis and a child born to her is blind from birth. A thief is placed into prison or given some other sort of punishment. A drunk driver and others in his accident end up in hospital. We could fill up pages concerning sins directly causing suffering to oneself and/or to others.

Although we know from Job that personal sin is not always the cause, still when suffering descends upon us there should be an honest self-evaluation. This pain may indeed be alerting us to something seriously wrong in our lives and it becomes a call to repentance. Our human nature is not too eager in regard to repentance, and our culture – often even our spiritual culture – tries to ignore it. Like Adam and Eve, when the Creator comes calling, we are too busy scrambling to hide ourselves, trying to evade any accountability. So often then the pain is necessary to bring out into the open the danger that we have caused particularly on the spiritual level. Only in this way can the garbage that clutters up our relationship with the Lord be removed.

This is not casual to God – He *pleads with*, not offhandedly mentions to – His People:

> Cast away from you all your transgressions by which you have rebelled, and form for yourselves a new heart and a new spirit. For why should you die, O house of Israel? Ezekiel 18:31

> "As I live," says the Lord Jehovah, "have I pleasure in the death of the wicked? Rather it be that the wicked turn from his way and live! Turn, turn from your evil ways – why should you die, O house of Israel?" Ezekiel 33:11

> O Jerusalem, Jerusalem, who kills the prophets and stones those who are sent to her! How often would I have gathered your children together as a hen gathers her chicks under the wings, and you were not willing! Matthew 23:37

The Lord is serious about His own People's choice to *not* reflect His Love: they do not care about the victims, the widows, the fatherless, and those who have been sold into slavery because of debt. The calloused enforced servitude of *their fellow Israelites* brings out a strong reaction from Jehovah, especially when they at first had set free these neighbors:

> "But you turned again and disgraced My Name, and every one caused his male and female slaves, whom you had set free to their delight, to return and brought them again into subjection ..."
> . Therefore thus says Jehovah: "You have not heeded Me in proclaiming freedom, every one to his brother and every one to his neighbor. Behold, I proclaim freedom to you, ... – to the sword, to pestilence, and to famine! I will set you as an object of trembling to all the kingdoms of the earth." Jeremiah 34:16-17

What stays God's hand for millennia? Why has He wasted so much time pleading with – begging – His People?

the Lord does not delay the promise as some may consider it as reluctance, but is patient toward you, not willing for any to perish but that all come to repentance.   II Peter 3:9

Here again is Love at work. His commitment to Love – and to have love in return – is that serious and that enduring. His desire is still to return humanity to the Image of God and to the eternal partnership for which He has designed us, and He will give them even extra time to repent.

The Suffering of the Forgiven

However, although the forgiveness which the Lord gives to the repentant is real and effective, a person may not be miraculously removed from the effects of the sin. Adam and Eve are forgiven (as indicated by the covering of skins from an innocent victim with its implied sacrifice [Genesis 3:21]), which would let them and their descendants know that such mercy is available through grace (hence the beginning the system of sacrifices as *God*'s act of forgiveness – *"I* have given it to you on the altar for making atonement for your Souls" [Leviticus 17:11]). Yet the universe has been changed: sin has now entered this *cosmos* and they will still experience suffering. So also, for example, the woman with syphilis does not suddenly cease to be infected when she repents.

Even "David the son of Jesse, a man after My own heart, who will do all My will" [Acts 13:22], although forgiven, could not escape the consequences of his adultery with Bathsheba and his subsequent murder of her husband [II Samuel 11] by simply repenting [12:13]. Yes, "Jehovah has taken away your sin; you shall not die" – so the eternal consequences are settled –, yet "However, because this deed has brought the enemies of Jehovah to contempt and to blaspheme, so the child will instead surely die" [v 14], which he does [v 18]. Another result of this sin would be:

Now the sword will always not depart from your house, for you have despised Me by taking the wife of Uriah the Hittite and she has become your wife, therefore thus says Jehovah, behold, I will raise up evil against you from your household. …   12:10-11

David would run for his life from his son Absalom's attempted coup [chapters 15 through 19].

It is reasonable that God would not withhold these results from sin because, as discussed earlier, so many other lives are entwined with David's: consider the effect on the nation if they observe sin unrestrained by any sort of discipline – as well as the effect on David himself if he discovers that he need not carry his earthly and spiritual position with responsibility. Truly, normally David's love of his Lord does restrain him, but as this incident reveals, there is still need for additional reminders of who he is and of his obligations to God and to others. As St Paul can attest, in the battle against our fallen human nature [Romans 7:14-25], we do need all the help we can get (and do get through the Holy Spirit).

Therefore even when there is such disciplinary results from sin, it is not punishment merely for the sake of retribution, it is not because the forgiveness hangs on a hair-breadth, but rather it is oriented to a goal of calling people to return to their Creator and His ways, since it actually does make life more bearable on this earth when the hand of evil is placed under restraint.

Hereditary and Collective Sin

Who can bring a clean thing out of an unclean? No one!   Job 14:4

This topic is truly strange to us because our western thinking is different than that which is in the Bible. We subscribe to the ideal of what might be called "the American Dream," a romantic model of an utterly independent pioneer on top of a hill surveying his land and his accomplishments and proclaiming, "I have built this all by myself!" That kind of an ideal will not stand under scrutiny, and yet we still glorify that rugged individualism – actually it is a reshaped desire to be like God, supremely self-sufficient and … self-centered. Therefore such a doctrine as "original sin," where we are placed by birth under Adam and Eve's sin, sounds at best awkward, if not offensive.

Collective Sin

To unravel this topic, it might be best to first talk about "collective sin," the sin which we share jointly because of our solidarity with each other in one form or another. Here the example of Achan may be of value: Jericho stands before the Israelites as the "door-opener" to the Promised Land, the first conquest, "the first fruits" of their new home, and as such it is to be totally "dedicated" to Jehovah [Joshua 6:17-19] – its plunder is not to be for the use of the People. However note the wording of chapter 7, verse 1:

> But *the children of Israel* acted with gross unfaithfulness regarding the dedicated things: Achan … of the tribe of Judah, took of the dedicated things; so the anger of Jehovah burned against *the children of Israel*.

When this miraculously victorious nation is defeated by the dinky little town of Ai, Joshua is told:

> *Israel* has sinned, indeed they have transgressed My Covenant which I commanded them: they have especially taken from the dedicated things – they have both stolen and deceived; and have even put it among their own possessions. Therefore *the children of Israel* could not stand before their enemies, … because they now have become "dedicated" – accursed. I will not be with you anymore, unless you destroy the dedicated thing from among you.   7:11-12

Ultimately,

> Did not Achan the son of Zerah act rebelliously in the dedicated thing, and wrath fell on all the congregation of Israel? Yet he did not perish alone in his iniquity.   22:20

The sin of taking to oneself what belongs to the Lord is a serious rebellion, and the ramifications are such that not only is the whole nation found accountable and guilty, so also soldiers are sacrificed on the battlefield and in the end his whole household is destroyed [7:24-26].

Another example is when David chooses to number His People in II Samuel 23:1-25 and I Chronicles 21:1-30 (in which both passages together almost echo the scene in heaven in Job 1 and 2). What is the king's sin, which Satan incited, we are not told, although Joab protested about its propriety. Still, it seems that David's pride is (again) a major player in this case yet the whole nation is subject to the penalty of the sin, a suffering which caused even Jehovah Himself to cry out, "Enough!" [II Samuel 23:16; I Chronicles 21:15] and David to repent [II Samuel 23:10, 17; I Chronicles 21:8, 17].

Collective Responsibility

The sense of collective responsibility does occur even in our modern age: Do we hold the German people accountable for the atrocities of the Nazi regime? Should the Japanese apologize to their victim countries? Should the United States apologize to families of former slaves? And what about reparations? If the wrongs of the past are to be righted, who is responsible (i.e., assumes the guilt)? An example of this can be found in II Samuel 21:

> There was a famine in the days of David for three years, year after year; and David sought the face of Jehovah. Jehovah answered, "It is because of Saul and his bloody house, because he killed the Gibeonites." …
> The Gibeonites said to him, "We will have neither silver nor gold from Saul or from his house, nor shall you kill any man in Israel for us."
> He said, "Whatever you say, I will do for you."
> They said to the king, "The man, who consumed us and who planned our annihilation from all the territory of Israel, let seven men, his sons – of Saul, the chosen of Jehovah – be given to us, so that we may hang them up before Jehovah at Gibeah."
> The king said, "I will give them." …

He gave them into the hands of the Gibeonites, and they hanged them on a hill before Jehovah. So all seven together fell, and were put to death ...   v 1, 4-6, 9

When Israel first settled the Land, the Gibeonites had by deception entered into Covenant with Israel [Joshua 9:3-27], a *forbidden* Covenant [Deuteronomy 7:1-2; 20:16-18]. However, any Covenant – even by deception – was not to be broken without the pain of death, yet Saul has broken this one by an attempted ethnic cleansing. The Lord as Overseer demands an accounting and the ball is in the Gibeonites' court – they could have held all Israel accountable life-for-life, but they only ask for seven of Saul's sons. Seven is the sole Hebrew number which is also a word, the word for the "oath" used in Covenant, so it seems that by the death of the seven sons, the broken Covenant is now restored.

So also, when Daniel is overcome by the realization of the sin of his People, his prayer of confession focuses not only on his own sin and unworthiness but also how these fall under the umbrella of all the accumulated sin which has brought about the Babylonian Captivity of Israel, as he takes responsibility to confess *all* of the sin:

I prayed to Jehovah my God and confessed, saying, "Alas, O Lord, ... *we* have sinned, committed iniquity, acted wickedly and rebelled, turning aside from Your commandments and ordinances; *we* have not listened to Your servants the prophets ... In the Lord our God there is mercy and forgiveness; but *we* have rebelled against Him, and have not obeyed Jehovah our God ... *we* have not been afflicted before the face of Jehovah our God, turning from *our* iniquities and giving heed to Your truth. ... *we* have sinned, *we* have acted wickedly. ... for it is not on account of our righteousness do *we* present our supplications before You, but on account of Your great mercy. O Jehovah, hear; O Jehovah, forgive; O Jehovah, heed and act..."
While I was speaking, praying and confessing *my sin and the sin of my People* Israel ... the man Gabriel ... came to me ...
Daniel 9:4-6, 9-10, 13, 15, 18-19, 20-21

Read the chapter and note how Daniel humbly acknowledges sins of commission, sins of omission, and especially sins against the warnings of God's Word and the entreaties of God's servants. The prophet is very explicit. He lays bare his heart before the Lord, tearing off every layer from the corruption of the people. He exposes the wound to the inspection of the Great Surgeon and asks Him to heal it. I believe that the Lord is about to bless the man who personally is given a deep sense of sin; and certainly the church that is willing to make confession of its own sinfulness and unworthiness is on the eve of a visitation of love.

Charles Spurgeon[49]

Why Collective Responsibility?

The Creator has not designed humanity to be a bunch of individuals, but rather a community, reflecting in a larger way, "it is not good that the man should be alone" [Genesis 2:18]. To understand this concept, perhaps a good place to begin is the idea of "It takes a whole village to raise a child," that is, everyone assumes responsibility for the welfare of the children (although not always should this be limited to the young):

> Proverb or not, "It takes a whole village to raise a child" reflects a social reality some of us who grew up in rural areas of Africa can easily relate to. As a child, my conduct was a concern of everybody, not just my parents, especially if it involved misconduct. Any adult had the right to rebuke and discipline me and would make my mischief known to my parents who in turn would also mete their own "punishment." The concern of course was the moral wellbeing of the community.
>
> Lawrence Bogoni[50]

> I have lived on three continents, in small towns, and funny, I found that the Belgian Ardennes villages, the Maniema villages (Zaire), and Kansas villages all behave in the same way: the affairs of one are the concern of all. If a child misbehaves, everybody will try to correct him or her, the story teller will keep them entertained, the teacher, the priest, the lady who is the best cook, all will participate with the parents, the extended family, and everybody else. As a correspondent said, this kind of education happened also in neighbourhoods in big cities.   Claire Dehon[51]

This is extended by the question Cain asks, "Am I my brother's keeper?" [Genesis 4:9]. Although he meant it to cover his murder of Abel, still the question has larger boundaries, as Jehovah declares to Ezekiel:

98

You, son of man, I have appointed as a watchman for the house of Israel; you will hear a word from my mouth and will warn them from me: when I say to the wicked, "O wicked one, you will surely die," and you do not speak to dissuade him from his ways, that wicked one will die for his sin, but I will hold you accountable for his Blood [Life/Soul]. But if you warn the wicked from his way, to turn from it, and he does not turn from his way; he will die in his iniquity, but you will have saved your life.   Ezekiel 33:7-9

Yes, this is addressed to Ezekiel, but if we consider Achan again, here is a man who leaves the Jericho ruins "pregnant," with the gold, silver and clothing hidden under his garment. Has nobody really noticed, or is it more the sin of turning a blind eye and of not confronting the person concerning the grave sin. The principle is in the New Testament:

Brothers, if a man is overtaken in any trespass, you, the spiritual ones, restore him in a spirit of gentleness, considering yourself, lest you too be tempted. Bear the burdens of one another, and so fulfill the law of Christ. Bear one another's burdens, and so fulfill the law of Christ. For if anyone thinks himself to be something while being nothing, he deceives himself. However let each one test his own work … For each will bear his own load.   Galatians 6:1-5

My brothers, if anyone among you wanders from the truth, and someone brings him back, let him know that he who brings backs a sinner from the error of his way will save his soul from death and cover a multitude of sins.   James 5:19-20

Reading Galatians and James, one might think that such responsibility to another is merely a casual option, should one have inclination and time, but looking at the communal responsibility in the Old Testament, the evidence is that there can be severe ramifications to such negligence. Now-a-days it may not result in an epidemic as in Israel's day – or maybe it just might. Or is it the progressive deterioration of the culture? At least with the epidemic there is the wake-up call of "pain," whereas the deterioration of the culture may be suffering the leprosy of creeping insensitivity to God's will, which can ultimately be even more lethal – eternally lethal.

There is another area into which our penitence should enter, the sin of the world. It is no sentimental theory which asserts that all men have responsibility towards the common sin of humankind. *The world's sin is our own sin.* We cannot passively acquiesce or treat it as inevitable. We share responsibility for it, and when we face that till it wounds and pains, then we are taking our proper place in the brotherhood of mankind. The misery and weariness of the world's sin becomes part of our own pain, so that the heart is filled with pity and with purpose to seek that saving grace be brought into contact with the sin of the world. Here, too, hopefulness and expectation are born. The sin of others is united with our penitence and with our experience of the loving-kindness and the saving mercies of Christ. We bring men penitence by repenting. We learn to hope for the world, because we have found boundless mercy towards ourselves and cannot despair for others.

George S. Steward[52]

Generational Sin

Not only is there such a thing as community suffering, there is also generational results of sin: "for I Jehovah am your God, a jealous God visiting the iniquity of the fathers upon the children unto the third and fourth generation of them who hate me" [Exodus 20:5; 34:7; Numbers 14:18]. In fact, Jesus even indicates that the tsunami of the accumulation of generations can descend upon an unrepentant generation as they reject God-come-into-flesh, Jesus:

> On account of this God's wisdom, 'I will send them prophets and apostles, and some of them they will kill and persecute,' in order that the blood of all the prophets poured out since the world's foundation would be required of this generation, from the blood of Abel to the blood of Zechariah who perished between the altar and the temple. Yes, I say to you, it will be required of this generation.   Luke 11:49 -51

Is there no way out of such a dire misfortune? Leviticus 26:40-42 makes an interesting statement about repentance in contrast:

> But if they confess their iniquity *and the iniquity of their fathers* – with their trespasses in which they rebelled against Me, and in which they also walked hostile to Me, … if their uncircumcised hearts become humble

100

and they accept their guilt – then I will remember My Covenant with Jacob, My Covenant with Isaac and My Covenant with Abraham I will remember; I will remember the Land.

When Nehemiah recounts, "on behalf of Your servants, the People of Israel, confessing the sins of the People of Israel, which we have sinned against You – I and my father's house have sinned" [1:6] and "they stood and confessed both their sins and the sins of their fathers" [9:2-3], as with Daniel (quoted above), more than just one's own sin must be called to account and resolved.

The irresponsibility of the father can cause the son to be condemned:

Every male child among you shall be circumcised... in the flesh of your foreskins, and it shall be a SIGN of the Covenant between Me and you. He that is eight days old among you shall be circumcised; every male throughout your generations ... , both he that is born in the house and he that is bought with money ..., shall be circumcised. So shall My Covenant be in your flesh an everlasting Covenant. An uncircumcised male who is not Circumcised in the flesh of his foreskin, his Soul/Life shall be cut off from his People; *he has broken My Covenant.*
Genesis 17:11-14

How "unfair"! How can it be said of an infant: "*he* has broken My Covenant"? Yet the omissions of the father cannot be justification for the son to dwell in disobedience. The responsibility of parenting is that the parent *can* bring effects upon one's offspring – and not just spiritually:

DNA damage induced by low x-ray doses persists longer than damage caused by high doses.[53]
...the psychoactive ingredient of marijuana (tetrahydrocannabinol-THC) is a fat-soluble molecule. ... THC metabolites are stored in the brain, testes, ovaries, and other fatty tissues. ... Higher doses of marijuana have been found to be sevenfold more mutagenic than either tobacco or low-dose marijuana (both of which were also, but more weakly, mutagenic).[54]

If a parent can cause physical genetic mutations which will affect future generations, so also the same happens spiritually. And in opposite character, even godly acts are shared with the offspring, as Hebrews 7:9-10 identifies:

> so to speak, through Abraham, even Levi, who receives tithes, paid tithes for he was still in the loins of his father when Melchizedek met him.

An ancestor has a continuing effect on future descendants: *corporate* and *personal* actions, attitudes, prejudices, rebellions (sin) get passed on to a child, which become part of a human nature "spiritually genetically" mutated. Therefore "Adam ... begot a son in his own likeness, after his image" [Genesis 5:3], rather than in "the likeness of God" [v 1]. This then sets up an important contrast in Romans and I Corinthians:

Romans 5:12-21

Adam

sin came into the world and death thru sin
death spread to all men (all men sinned)
many died through one man's trespass
judgment following one trespass brought condemnation
because of one man's trespass, death reigned through that one man
one man's trespass led to condemnation for all men
by one man's *disobedience* many made sinners

Jesus

God's grace abounded for many
the free gift following many trespasses brings justification
the abundance of grace and free gift of righteousness reign in life
the one man righteousness leads to acquittal and life for all men
by one man's obedience many made righteous
grace might reign thru righteousness to life

I Corinthians 15:21-22, 45, 49

Adam

by a man came death
in Adam all die
the first man Adam became a living being
we have borne the image of the man of dust

102

Jesus

by a man came the resurrection of the dead
in Christ shall all be made alive
the last Adam became a life-giving spirit
we will bear the image of the man of heaven

When St Paul sets Adam and Jesus into parallel, it means that an effect applied to one side must also apply to the other, therefore:

If Adam merely sets a precedent, then Jesus merely sets a precedent.

If humanity is condemned because it *imitates* Adam, then salvation would come only because humanity *imitates* Jesus (e.g., "one man's obedience").

If salvation comes because "*in* Christ" righteousness is *received personally* from Jesus, then death comes because "*in* Adam" condemnation is *received personally* from Adam.   James Lindemann[55]

One verse often used against the view that Adam's sin is imputed to us is Ez. 18.20: "The person who sins will die. The Son will not bear the punishment for the father's iniquity. ...." Note carefully that the passage's context is not about federal representation, but of a law-abiding person not being held guilty for the sin of a family member. In other words, it is a judicial matter among the Israelites. Nevertheless, however one interprets this passage one thing is certain, Ez. 18.20 does allow for exceptions, otherwise Christ cannot bear our sins, and we are left to make ourselves right with God by our own futile efforts.

Michael Bremmer[56]

Because of our modern individualism, if we are too quick to dismiss the idea of corporate and generational sin, we then weaken particularly the blessings of salvation from Jesus, as well as the understanding, for example, of how Israel goes off into captivity due to the repeated and accumulated rebellions which have marked their history.

Have a Good Day

Considering how earthly effects of sin can remain even after one receives Jehovah's forgiveness, and also when one considers the effect of community sin and generational sin, along with Satan's devices constantly targeting us, the reality is that often we do *not* suffer even a small part of what our sin should bring. The comment has been made that it is not the bad day that should be so unique, rather we should be amazed that we would ever have a "good" day! Of such is the mercy and grace of the Lord.

And there is another reason for a "good day": returning to Luke 11:49-51 as quoted above, "the blood of all the prophets poured out since the world's foundation would be required of this generation" is fulfilled in one sense by the terrible fall of Jerusalem by Roman hands in 70 AD, however there is a way out from under such condemnation. One "of this generation" takes upon Himself the full judgment of all the blood spilled from Abel onward: Jesus. Again there is a dual result as Corrie, Betsy and Gordon would come to understand: even though the horror of the world's circumstances surround them, spiritually they are lifted to another world in which its realities provide the hope which cannot be taken from them – it is "a living hope through the resurrection of Jesus Christ from the dead" [I Peter 1:3]. Therefore one can speak of "a good day" even while suffering in the extreme.

Unfortunately, we begin to depend on such mercy from God as an excuse to get away with something "this time," be it speeding or some other usual "bending of the rules" – similar to the potent danger of insensitivity to one's responsibilities as David faced in regard to the Bathsheba incident. The prophets have much to say about such a cavalier attitude toward God's mercy, as they warned their hearers that if they persist in this kind of rebellion, they can be saving up an accumulation of justice that one day will break upon them, and it can be as harsh as a Babylonian Captivity, or as terrible as the result of the Jews rejection of Jesus. Yet even in the midst of such judgment, the Lord does not desert them, does not destroy them, but rather still seeks the ultimate result of a stronger connection between Him and those who would be His People.

7. Innumerable Tasks

As a tool in the hands of the Creator, we realize that suffering can have many different tasks, but it may be a surprise to discover how many such tasks occur simultaneously in any given episode – remember just how wide the net of suffering can be cast!

Unique Wisdom

As Jesus responds to the disciples' question, "Rabbi, who sinned, this man or his parents, that he was born blind?" [John 9:3], the answer is that *nothing* they did brought it on. No great sin has compelled God to act in judgment: no parental indiscretion, no unforgivable "bad karma" (not even from so-called "past lifetimes") has put a dark cloud on this man's life, and no future sin has caused this suffering. We know from Job that there are many other factors that figure into suffering than merely punishment.

The man in John 9 understands that his blindness is just something he has to bear – after all, as he himself states, "throughout the ages, it was never heard that anyone opened the eyes of one blind from birth" [v 32]. But this particular blindness has an essential role, not just in its healing, but in giving a wisdom upon which an iron-clad logical deduction could be made. Jesus uses clay on the man's eyes, which has to be washed off elsewhere so that even after being healed – he would still be "blind" about Who or what Jesus is. The man's conclusions come from what his *blindness* taught him: the only One Who could heal such a handicap from birth must have God's hand upon Him – his experience of suffering equipped him to use powerful logic to refute the sighted blindness of the Pharisees.

Suffering helps us realize that which is important and necessary, and a handicap may actually be of benefit. Frazier Hunt once spoke of feeling dejected and discouraged during a dry spell in his writing as he rode his horse on his regular call to Helen Keller, the famous deaf and blind woman. He had his horse stand as he watched Helen walking alone by following a smooth wire that had been stretched for her through a wooded area. She stopped and gathered a handful of wolf willows, breathing in their fragrance, then with her face toward the warm sun, mouthed the word, "Beautiful!" Frazier had tears in his eyes. He could see all the wonders of the world and sky, he could hear all the sounds of nature around him, yet he had been so preoccupied with his problems he missed it all. It took someone who could neither see nor hear to show him beauty and courage.

Pruned

> Burrowing into his past, [C.S. Lewis] was appalled at what he found...
> "I have found out ludicrous and terrible things about my own character.
> Sitting by, watching the rising thoughts to break their necks as they pop
> up, one learns to know the sort of thoughts that do come. And, will you
> believe it, one out of every three is a thought of self-admiration: when
> everything else fails (having had its neck broken), up comes the thought
> 'What an admirable fellow I am to have broken their necks!' ... I catch
> myself posturing before the mirror, so to speak, all day long. I pretend I
> am carefully thinking out what to say to the next pupil (for his good, of
> course) and then suddenly realize I am really thinking how frightfully
> clever I'm going to be and how he will admire me.... when you force
> yourself to stop it, you admire yourself for doing that. It's like fighting
> the hydra... There seems to be no end to it. Depth under depth of self-
> love and self-admiration... Pride ... is the mother of all sins, and the
> original sin of Lucifer."   Roger Lancelyn[57]

In John 15, Jesus describes Himself as the Vine, we as the branches, His Father as the vinedresser, and that "every branch that bears fruit He prunes, that it may bear more fruit" [v 2]. CS Lewis identified that there needs to be a constant maintenance of the little "sucker shoots" of sin which plague us, which continuously divert our energies and attention from the God-declared task of being His reflection, His Image, on this earth.

But pruning does not always deal with useless or non-productive growth – many times it is a choice of decreasing the quantity of fruit so that what remains can reach its fullest potential. When we look down and see on the ground that pruned branch which had flourishing fruit, we can be upset – in other words, where we think we have a talent or ability, now the situation has arisen where we cannot give it the time and effort we may have wanted. Instead we find ourselves led in a different direction, one which can be a more difficult path or one not quite what we had wanted at first.

Other times we see on the ground branches that have been reliable and productive for years – in other words, we have been able to use our abilities in worthwhile and God-pleasing ways, only to find that we have lost the ability in some way. This is often the experience of the aged as strength, eyes, ears, finger mobility and other weaknesses set in, or those of any age where a major incident has left them without use of arms, legs, speech or whatever it may be. Having such diminished capacity, the question often is raised by such a person as to what worth and value have they now – what possible fruit can they have now?

In perhaps the worst scenarios, dementia has set in and the branch seems to be stripped of any "fruit-producing" ability; or, in a wider application, a congregation has lost one of its best and most versatile irreplaceable workers.

A bewildered question asks just what is it for which the Vinedresser is looking – so much of previous "fruit" had been done in a genuine desire to serve Him! Does He not realize how He has crippled His own goals (for example, "make disciples of all nations")? What is it which is so important to Him that He would do such radical pruning?

A starting place for an answer is to look at the "fruit of the Spirit":

But the fruit of the Spirit is love, joy, peace, longsuffering, kindness, goodness, faithfulness, gentleness, self-control. ...   Galatians 5:22-23

We often naturally assume that the fruit the Vinedresser is seeking is some sort of accomplishments, yet the description here is of qualities and attitudes. Perhaps surprisingly, these fruit have similarity to Jehovah's own definition of His Glory in Exodus 33 and 34: goodness, Covenant relationship, grace, mercy, Steadfast Love, faithfulness, forgiveness and justice. The odd thing about these fruit is that even a person with dementia can exhibit at least some of them. Possibly then, the reason for the pruning is far different from what we normally expect: it is to develop and expose spiritual qualities, not so much an accumulation of deeds; and also to draw us closer to the Source of this kind of Life:

I am the Vine, you are the branches – he who remains in Me and I in him bears much fruit, for apart from Me you can do nothing. ... You did not choose Me, but I chose you that you should go and bear fruit, and that your fruit should endure...   John 15:5, 16

We have been grafted into the main stem [Romans 11:17-18] by the Lord's grace, but the graft is not without suffering: on the Cross the Vine is cut and His Life flows. Through His Word, His Sacraments, His Church; through worship, prayer, the sharing of "faith, hope and love" [I Corinthians 13:13] among His People, the Lifeblood surges into our lives and we become *enthusiastic* ("enthusiasm" comes from the Greek "en theou" – "in God"). All sorts of changes happen in us, qualities and attitudes are transformed, the fruit grows – and not only is this "much fruit," in verse 16 it has the ring of eternity to it.

It is comforting to also know that Jesus is Himself a "Branch", the Branch of Jesse [Isaiah 11:1], and He knows full well how pruning involves *pain*, deliberate and necessary pain. He has not been immune to the pain of frustration, of weakness, of inability, of being victim, even to Himself being "cut off" [Isaiah 53:8; Daniel 9:26]. Yet He is also David's "'Branch of Righteousness': a King to reign and prosper, and to execute judgment and righteousness in the earth" [Jeremiah 23:5; 33:15], Who is on "the Throne of Grace, that we may receive mercy and find grace for timely help" [Hebrews 4:16]. How good it is to have this Source Who provides the resources for our "much fruit … which will endure."

Refining (Exposing and Empowering)

> You weren't a decent man and you didn't do your best. We none of us were and none of us did.   CS Lewis[58]

Whereas "pruning" can be the removing what can also be good and healthy in order to promote the desired fruit, "refining" both removes what contaminates the purity and brings out the beauty of something precious (a metal).

Refining can be painful, yet Jehovah is not afraid of it – it can be the wedge that breaks through the complacency of daily life; the catalyst that exposes what is real and basic in especially spiritual life, as St Paul discovers:

> Wherefore that I may not be exalted ... a messenger of Satan to torment me … Three times I begged the Lord that it might be removed from me, but He said to me, "My grace is sufficient for you, for indeed power is perfected in weakness." Most gladly therefore will I rather boast in my weaknesses, that the power of Christ may dwell upon me.
> II Corinthians 12:7-9

Paul's appeal to the Lord likely was no offhand remark, but rather pleading, arguing and crying out to be rid of what he saw as a hindrance. But Jesus turns it around and says that this harassment is – as pain is – actually an asset, it will keep their relationship active and living and ultimately will reveal God's power in him. Like Corrie, Betsy and the Kwai prisoners in the death camps, Paul realizes that the power lies not so much in the accumulation of deeds nor in what is comfortable, but rather in the spiritual relationship which gives Life, meaning and ability to those who suffer.

However, as CS Lewis confessed at the beginning of the last section, it is not so much the big problems but the little niggling sins of daily life which often can prove so wearisome and problematic for Paul:

> I do not understand my own actions. For I do not do what I want, but I do the very thing I hate. Now if I do what I do not want, I agree that the law is good. So then it is no longer I that do it, but sin which dwells within me. For I know that nothing good dwells within me, that is, in my flesh. I can will what is right, but I cannot do it. For I do not do the good I want, but the evil I do not want is what I do. Now if I do what I do not want, it is no longer I that do it, but sin which dwells within me. So I find it to be a law that when I want to do right, evil lies close at hand. ... Wretched man that I am! Who will deliver me from this body of death? Thanks be to God through Jesus Christ our Lord! ...
>
> Romans 7:15-21, 24-25

Our difficulty with God's refining is that He is not interested in making us more able to control ourselves. Paul complains bitterly that whatever he does, in spite of being the extraordinary believer that he is, in spite of his best of intentions, everything must go through "this body of death" and the outcome is never as noble as he wishes. Ultimately he ends up thankfully throwing himself upon the grace and mercy of Jesus to deliver him.

Whereas pruning deals more with the spiritual fruit which reflects the Image of God (the One Who ultimately is to fill our vision), the refining's task is to draw out and reveal faith:

> ... in order that the testing of your faith – more precious than gold which perishes – though tested by fire, may be found to praise and glory and honor in the revealing of Jesus Christ   I Peter 1:7

110

It can be a faith which sometimes cannot be fully seen except through extraordinary trial, as articulated in what Jesus went through: "He learned/ *demonstrated* obedience through what He suffered" [Hebrews 5:8]; a faith which becomes a beacon to bring others to God's concrete help and hope, as the inmates of the death camps grow to understand in the midst of their suffering, and as Corrie discovers in her subsequent ministry:

> Corrie Ten Boom was not looking forward to her turn to speak. She and the others in her ministry team had gone to a prison to talk to the inmates about Christ. They had set up their equipment at one end of a long corridor lined with cells. The men peered through the bars to see the visitors.
> First, a woman sang, and the prisoners tried to drown her out. Then, when a young man stood to pray, the noise grew worse. Finally, it was Corrie's turn. Shouting to be heard, she said, "When I was alone in a cell for four months..." Suddenly, the corridor grew quiet. With those few words, Corrie established a bond with the prisoners. They realized that she knew what they were going through. Her time in a World War II prison camp made her one of them.   Unknown

It is a faith which is the badge of participation in Christ's work on earth:

> giving thanks to the Father who has made us competent to have a portion in the inheritance of the saints in the light. ... I now rejoice in suffering for you, and I fill up in my flesh what is lacking in the afflictions of Christ, on behalf of His Body, which is the Church
> Colossians 1:12, 24

"What is lacking in the affliction of Christ" is startling – can there be something unfinished in Jesus' work? The answer is "yes!" In the mystery of being partners, key players, with the Creator in bringing His salvation to the *cosmos*, since the full invasion into Satan's territory ("disciples of all nations" [Matthew 28:19; Luke 24:47] and "preach the Gospel to the whole Creation" [Mark 16:15]) is not completed, there is no one else to do this task but we humans, we believers. We therefore, as "participants in the sufferings, so also we will partake of the consolation" [II Corinthians 1:7], are exposed to the same rejection and ridicule, the same hatred and battle as Jesus experienced, and yet it is with an air of expectation:

> Do not be bewildered at the fiery test ... as if something unusual were happening. But rejoice because as you share Christ's sufferings, so also may you rejoice in delight in the revealing of His Glory. ... Resist [Satan], solid in the faith, knowing that the same sufferings are being experienced by your brethren in the world. Moreover, the God of all grace, the One Who called you to His eternal Glory in Christ Jesus, after you have suffered a little while, equip, establish, strengthen, and ground you.   I Peter 4:12-13; 5:9-10

Our participation is such an enormously key role, that easily we may think that we must plunge in with our good intentions and ideas, only to be reminded by Paul (above) that this involves the frustration of going through "this body of death" [Romans 7:15-24]. The refining teaches us not to do things on our own, but instead as Paul must do, thankfully throwing ourselves upon the Lord, discovering how we are "His handiwork, created in Christ Jesus for good works, which God prepared previously that we should walk in them" [Ephesians 2:10]. The choice between our will and His is reflected in the "wood, hay, straw" or "gold, silver, precious stones" – the "valuables" upon which we "build" our spiritual houses, the "valuables" which will be tested by fire:

> For another foundation can no one lay besides that which is laid, which is Jesus Christ. Now if anyone builds upon the foundation with gold, silver, precious stones, wood, hay, straw, the work of each will become manifest; for the day will declare it, since in fire it will be revealed; and the fire itself will examine of what sort each's work is. If anyone's work which he has built remains, he will receive a reward. If anyone's work is consumed, he will suffer loss; although he himself will be saved, yet as through fire.
> Do you not know that you are the temple of God and that the Spirit of God dwells in you?   I Corinthians 3:11-16

Although "the day" likely refers to the Last Day (especially with the comment about still being saved), one wonders if the fire of refining can be found in whenever our faith is severely challenged, whether it be in the extremes in which the prisoners of the death camps found themselves or it be in the confrontation with modern philosophies and religious opinions. Many times, when a person's faith is grounded not on firsthand familiarity with the Bible, such challenges can be a very searing experience, oft times leaving the faith in burned-out ruins. Now comes the call to start rebuilding with the more lasting material.

Yet the very real comfort is that the Holy Spirit is God's declaration that *He* is also "full partner" to what we experience, that despite the pain of the refining, the Spirit is His "downpayment" or "earnest" living *inside our hearts*, evidence on how the Lord cannot abuse us nor forget us, since *He* will be affected as much as it affects us. We therefore, growing in sensitivity to His will both in His Word and in His community of the faithful, seek not so much the accumulation of deeds but rather the participation in His Glory, bearing the fruit of the Spirit's presence within us.

"Before I was afflicted I went astray; but now I keep Your word; … It is good for me that I was afflicted, so that I might learn Your statutes" [Ps 119:67, 71], one effect of such refining, within the Love which stands behind it, is the realization of what the success of it has now brought into one's life. Hezekiah would affirm, "Behold, peace [SHALOM] was bitter to me, very bitter; yet You loved my soul from the pit of destruction, You have cast all my sins behind Your back" [Isaiah 38:17].

Taking up the Cross Daily [Luke 9:23]

The Cross signifies the kind of suffering which Jesus endured because He was God's presence in this world, and is not merely some problem in life no matter how tough it may be. What is novel about this topic is the emphasis on our choice to "take up" the Cross and follow Him.

Actually, "taking up" some sort of suffering is not unusual – athletes do it all the time as they choose to be inconvenienced and, even worse, to physically and socially suffer for the sake of their goal. Some people who are handicapped choose to struggle against hardship and pain, determined to maintain or regain their way of life rather than to give in to helplessness. Some students, in order to achieve proficiency in a career, choose to place themselves into great debt, forgoing the "freer" lifestyles of others. Parents have chosen great sacrifices in order to advance their children.

When Jesus tells us, "If anyone wishes to come after Me, let him deny himself, take up his cross each day, and let him follow Me." [Luke 9:23], this is no masochistic needless suffering just to wear a badge of pain. No mere inconvenience, the Cross of Jesus may make one end up in a death camp, as it did Martin Niemöller and Dietrich Bonhoffer and many other Christian martyrs and sufferers throughout history. It is not the ache of arthritis, or a string of "bad luck," or uncooperative children, although the Cross may be found in how we choose to react to such things. It is something which we "take up each day," a lifestyle entwined with following our Lord, not merely in being a "nice" person, but rather in how we will conform to God's will. This is not easy – Jesus makes some strong statements, as an example:

> Love your enemies, do nobly to those who hate you, bless those who curse you, and pray for those who spitefully abuse you. To him who strikes you on the one cheek, offer the other also; and from him who takes away your cloak, do not withhold your tunic also. Give to everyone who asks of you; and from him who takes away your goods do not ask for it back. ...
> If you love those who love you, what credit is that to you? For even sinners love those who love them. If you do good to those who do good to you, what credit is that to you? For even sinners do the same. If you lend to those from whom you hope to receive, what credit is that to you? For even sinners lend to sinners to receive the same in return.
> But Love your enemies, do good, and lend, not at all despairing; your reward will be great, and you will be sons of the Most High, for He is kind to the ungrateful and evil. You be compassionate, just as your

114

Father also is compassionate. Judge not, and you shall not be judged; condemn not, and you shall not be condemned. Forgive, and you will be forgiven.   Luke 6:27-37

These are hard things by themselves, but the "kicker" is that they often come with people of whom we are not very fond. What is particularly bothersome is the idea that we "will be sons of the Most High, for He is kind to the ungrateful and evil." Yes, it is nice to be part of a special class of humanity, "children of the Most High," however, such humbling of ourselves before those we consider undesirable is quite uncomfortable and distasteful – our human nature screams out how all this is really a stupid idea.

This is a "Cross" – at "cross-purposes" to the direction of our natural inclinations – in God's will: we become at risk; vulnerable; open to abuse; appearing very foolish and weak even to the person with whom we are dealing. It can be painful, not so much physically, but mentally, emotionally and even spiritually. Are there not sacrifices such things demand: will we not be less, have less, especially in those things which are "important"? Do we not have our dignity and integrity to uphold? Yet the focus of the Cross is not on the immediate difficulty, but rather on the endpoint objective, as Paul indicates in Hebrews 12:1: "having laid aside every weight and the easily distracting sin, let us run with endurance the race that is lying before us" The goal is well worth it, although *being convinced* that it is worth the effort and even the pain can be a challenge.

Important in this is Who bids us to take up our Cross. In Jesus we encounter not just a wise and very experienced Person, more than that, He has joined Himself to us in Baptism and Holy Communion. Therefore He knows and feels our suffering, already involved in our own "Crosses" with a depth of understanding which we will never fully comprehend. There is a Strength and a Hope to which we can turn, as He puts His shoulder under our burden [Psalm 55:22; I Peter 5:7], "we know that for those who love

115

God, He works all things together for good" [Romans 8:28]. In fact, we even discover the resource and effects of His Love already *in us*:

> Not only that, but we also boast in tribulations, knowing that tribulation produces steadfastness; and steadfastness, tested character; and tested character, hope, and the hope does not humiliate us, because God's Love has been poured into our hearts through the Holy Spirit Who has been given to us   Romans 5:3-5

Although we fear "With men it is impossible," Jesus continues, "but not with God; for with God all things are possible" [Mark 10:27].

We do have God's involvement and His promise "that the One having begun a good work in you will complete it up to the Day of Jesus Christ" [Philippians 1:6]. In other words, the goal toward which we are moving, He will back up its success – it will be worth the sacrifice and suffering to receive "to the prize of the high calling of God in Christ Jesus" [Philippians 3:14] and His "Well done, good and faithful servant; you were faithful over a few things, I will set you over many things; enter into the joy of your Master" [Matthew 25:21].

"Righteous" vs "Good" – Doing What is Right

> Therefore they who suffer according God's will, let them commit their souls to a faithful Creator in doing good   I Peter 4:19

"Taking up the Cross" means doing what Jesus desires, even when it is against our nature. But this section deals with the suffering that comes from *the world* because one has done what is godly:

> Servants, be subject to your masters with all respect, not only to the good and fair, but also to the twisted – this is indeed acceptable, if because of conscience toward God anyone endures grief, suffering unjustly. For what credit is it if when you sin and are struck you bear up under it? But if when doing good and suffering, and you bear up under it, this is proof of grace before God.

116

For to this you have been called, because Christ suffered for you, leaving to you an example, that you should follow in His steps. "Who committed no sin, nor was treachery found in His mouth"; Who, when He was abused, did not abuse in return; when He suffered, He did not threaten, but gave Himself over to Him Who judges righteously; Who Himself bore our sins in His body on the tree, that, having died to sin, we might live for righteousness – from whose wounds you were healed.

I Peter 2:18-24

Of course, Jesus is the prime example of not doing anything wrong yet still suffering. In a very glaring manner, this is brought out when not even the false witnesses could make a *false* accusation stick [Matthew 26:59-63; Mark 14:56-59]. Just why is a person who has done no wrong condemned by the world? St Paul provides an interesting turn of phrase in Romans 5:7: "Rarely will anyone die for a righteous man – though on behalf of a good man one perhaps might dare to die…" What is the difference between "a righteous man" and "a good man" – and why the reluctance toward the "righteous man"?

Something about "a righteous man" just rubs us against the grain. Perhaps back in school there was the "goody-two-shoes," the person who actually made everyone else look bad because he was just such an always good and responsible person. It was not necessarily that he was being obnoxious, in fact, he may have simply been doing and being what the Lord wanted us to do and to be. And we just could not stand him.

Yet we could not find that much with which to fault him – not that we did not try, as we would describe him as a fool and a jerk, so naïve and innocent – but basically it boiled down to the fact that he was the way we just did not want to be. He was "too religious," "too holy," and what not else, even though he may not have been "flaunting" his faith as much as we were rejecting it. Most likely we made life a hell for him, often with a giggle and even a crusader's mission to show just how stupid he really was. How

117

similar was our attitude to that of the Chief Priest and the rest of the leaders had when they condemned Jesus – but, of course, we will never admit it.

On the other hand, there is the "good man" – perhaps not quite as far as "a good ol' boy" but not that far away from it either. Here is someone who would not mind having "a little fun" now and then. Yet he is a decent sort of chap with both feet on the ground, and could be depended upon for whatever the occasion may require.

Now *he* would be one that we might die for, but "goody-two-shoes"? Naw, it would be a "tragedy" should the Lord take him, but then, we would glad to give him to the Lord, as long as he does not bother us any more. That may be crudely put, but often we are relieved when such a one leaves our presence. Paul, indeed, rightly understood our human nature when he makes the distinction between "a righteous man" and "a good man."

This is not God's fault, but rather it describes just how much the world is out of balance because of sin. Our human nature is just too much in rebellion with God to be comfortable with anything that comes close what God wants. After all, we just know that He wants to spoil all our fun.

How hard it is for the "righteous person," as he seeks to follow the will of the Lord, knowing that he will not fit in with what the world delights in, and knowing that every time he sticks to the Lord, that it will bring a varying degree of ridicule and even suffering.

St Peter understands this from when he is beaten for doing exactly what the Lord tells him to do [Acts 5:19-42], as he rejoices to be "counted worthy to suffer shame for [Jesus'] Name" [v 41]. Paul, as well, understands this from his missionary journeys when his life is threatened [for example, Acts 14:5, 19; 16:22-24] simply because he is doing what the Lord commands him to do [Acts 13:2-3]. In fact, Jesus indicates that as we approach the end times, the magnitude of this kind of suffering will increase dramatically.

All these are a beginning of the birth pains. Then they will deliver you to tribulation and kill you, and you will be hated by all nations on account of My Name. Many will be scandalized, they will betray one another and will hate each other. Many false prophets will rise up and lead many astray. Because lawlessness will multiply, the Love of many will grow cold, but the one who endures to the end shall be saved.

Matthew 24:8-13

The comfort for the "righteous man" is the awareness not only that such suffering is predicted, but that he simply is following in the footsteps, not just of Peter and Paul, but especially of the One Who was crucified by human hands, but has risen from the dead to demonstrate that the final outcome of such faithfulness is eternal life. And there is the promise that for some, they will recognize the presence of Jehovah as displayed by His People "in the day of visitation," which may not necessarily be the Last Day:

having your conduct honorable among the Gentiles, that when they speak against you as evildoers, through your good works which they witness, they might glorify God in the day of visitation.   I Peter 2:12

"Necessary" Evil

In college, in an argument with another student, this writer had taken the position that if there are only two choices, the "better" one is the God-pleasing one. The other fellow pointed out, that although it was "better," it did not necessarily make it godly – the Lord may not necessarily be "pleased" with it. He got nowhere in making his point. Finally as we separated, he said, "I'll pray for you." The arrogance of that comment!! But he must have prayed for me anyway, because he was correct.

What a world we live in! Even when we do what God instructs, we still can break His Law – note:

Have you not read in the law that on the Sabbath the priests in the temple break the Sabbath, and are guiltless?   Matthew 12:5

119

> Because of this Moses gave you Circumcision (not that it is from Moses, but from the fathers), and on the Sabbath you circumcise a man. If a man receives Circumcision on the Sabbath so that the law of Moses should not be broken, are you angry with Me because I made a whole man healthy on the Sabbath?   John 7:22-23

There is a tension in the first quote: Israel must worship God; yet the priests must break the Sabbath rule of doing no work, if the sacrifices are to be offered. The same problem occurs in the second quote with circumcising on the Sabbath. Of course the priests have permission to fulfill their duties, some of which can only be done on the Sabbath, and yet from a different angle, this still breaks God's Law. Also consider an interesting source of guilt in regard to the High Priest's function:

> Over his forehead is "Holy to Jehovah" [Exodus 28:36], and he will "bear the iniquity of the sacred things" [28:38][59]; "You ... shall bear the sanctuary's iniquity; and you ... shall bear your priesthood's iniquity ..." [Numbers 18:1,3,5]. In the sacrifices and in interceding, the LORD would call the priests to account.   James Lindemann[60]

"The iniquity of the sacred things," "the sanctuary's iniquity," "your priesthood's iniquity" – these are strange ideas to us. How can doing the tasks Jehovah sets before them have iniquity? Are they not doing what is "right," and yet somehow it is wrong? Apparently yes.

This is not a two-mindedness on God's part, but rather that now since rebellion has entered the universe, of such is the lot of everything which dwells in it. "So I find it to be a law that when I want to do right, evil lies close at hand" [Romans 7:21] – St Paul really knows of what he is speaking. Evil indeed is that close, even when doing the work of Jehovah. On the surface it is right, but at the deepest level, it is wrong: for example, the substitutionary deaths of the animals, and ultimately of Jesus, just should not be – this is not really the Lord's delight (I Samuel 15:22; Psalm 51:16; Isaiah

1:11-13), this should not have to be, something is *wrong* with this picture – and yet it is necessary because of sin.

At first we may simply pass this off as a trivial philosophical point, but actually there is a real suffering involved. Perhaps the most pronounced would be found in those who in the line of their work must take a life, such as a police officer or a soldier. One retired policeman mentioned that the only time he had to use his service revolver was to kill a pack of frenzied dogs which threatened a home. There was utter distaste in his features as he spoke about what he had to do, and he could not be more grateful that the gun never had to be used against a human. Many veterans of the wars have been strongly reluctant to talk about their time in the service, many still live with nightmares, many constantly have a shadow in the background of their days. This has none of the casual attitude toward killing which often fills so much of television and movies, but rather that to the very depths of our conscience, there is something wrong despite when taking life is necessary. This attitude can be seen in "primitive" cultures which often have a ceremony of asking permission and of apology to the animals which they will be hunting.

It can be a tension that can show up, for example, as when a parent must discipline a child, not so much in terms of corporal punishment, but particularly in the distaste of having to do something that just should not need to be done: it is the tension of doing what is right, necessary, sometimes unavoidable, and even godly – yet there is just something wrong with the picture. It is a suffering which humbles us and reminds us of how we live in a universe which desperately needs the intervention of its Creator and ultimately His re-creation to "make all things new" [Revelation 21:5].

When You Hate Your Job (Jeremiah Again)

In Ecclesiastes, Solomon declared,

> ... my heart rejoiced from all my labor; this became my reward from all my labor ... Is it not good for a man that he should eat and drink, and that his soul should see good in his labor? this also, I perceived, was from the hand of God   2:10, 24

> I know that it is not good for them but to rejoice and to do good in one's life, moreover every man should eat and drink and see good in all his labor – it is the gift of God.   3:12-13

Ah, yes, to enjoy "the good in his labor." Even in the secular press, we are told to find the jobs that we enjoy, because it makes our lives pleasant, it makes us eager to start the day, it makes us feel like we accomplish something worthwhile. Even Solomon says that this "is the gift of God."

But then, when Adam and Eve sinned, Jehovah declares that humanity would experience "toil" [Genesis 3:17-19]. "Toil" has been described as when, even though one may enjoy his work, there are times when it is not enjoyable, and yet one must keep on going, there is no choice – that is "toil." The gross expression of this would be slavery – it doesn't matter whether you do not like what you do, you must do it.

> Which of you, having a slave who is plowing or herding sheep, who has come in from the field, will say to him, "Come at once and sit at the table"? Rather will you not say to him, "Prepare what I will eat, gird yourself and serve me, till I eat and drink; and after this you will eat and drink"? Are you thankful to the slave because he did what was commanded? Thus you also, when you have done all which was commanded you, say, "We are unworthy slaves – we have done only what was required."   Luke 17:7-10

There was one person – and not even a "slave"! – who hated his job. Although we are not told what his mornings were like, probably when the alarm went off, he would yell at the rooster to shut up and would bury his head under the pillows. As he went off to work, it was not with a bright and cheery step, but rather with an effort to put one foot before the other.

He didn't even know when – and if – he would be home that evening.[61]

He wanted to resign, but it was just not allowed.[62]

He got no respect for what he was faithfully doing each day – his popularity was nil.[63]

He hated the work that he had to do, it was one of the most rotten of the "dirty jobs."[64] It was not as if he did lousy work – he did exactly what he was told to do – yet his supervisors were stuck in a dilemma: either make his life a living hell, or just kill him.[65]

His name was Jeremiah – "the weeping prophet" – and he is the sum total of the last sections.

Despite "the health, wealth and happiness gospel" promoters, Jeremiah *is* close to the Lord, he *is* faithfully following the Lord, fully obedient. He bravely faces the nation, his own People, doing and declaring exactly as Jehovah directs him. Everything that some believe should automatically bring on "the good life" is done by this prophet, but he is not happy, nor wealthy, and he might even have ulcers. He is *very* acquainted with "Suffering is the agony of living." Still Jeremiah faithfully does his job.

It would be nice if we did not have to remain in situations which we really do not like, yet sometimes there is no choice allowed. One may have to "settle" for any job available, even if it is not the one desired. Other times people who surround us simply want to make our life miserable, no matter how good a job we do. Some in the history of faith have been martyred – really or figuratively, ancient or modern – because of jealousy and other types of vendettas (just think of how many years Joseph ended up in prison [Genesis 39:20-23]).

Jeremiah can tell you that these things really happen.

Truly, if a better or more enjoyable setting is available, then run to it! But many of us are left with trying to find sense, purpose and hope in situations which we just do not like. What then are we to do? Jeremiah simply does what the Lord wants him to do, despite the circumstances. Joseph also maintained his integrity despite being sold into slavery [Genesis 38:23-30] and unfairly being thrown into prison [39:7-20].

Both Jeremiah and Joseph, though, present a contrast worthwhile to ponder. With Jeremiah, things do not ever go well, whereas with Joseph, he is blessed, successful, and literally ends up on top of everything. Why this difference? Why cannot one simply proscribe an outcome that works in all situations, as the "health, wealth and happiness gospel" attempts to do? God does not give us such a magic formula – each occasion is treated individually, case-by-case; each tailored to achieve an outcome necessary in His design for that time and place.

It would be nice to be Joseph – although consider the years he spent probably thinking that his were "dead end jobs." But think also of the slaves in the American South prior to the civil war, who lived, most frequently suffered, and died in such "dead end jobs." Like Job who is never told why he has to suffer as he does, it is doubtful that most of the slaves ever understood why they should endure their affliction. Yet as the "spirituals" (songs) give evidence, they maintained faith in spite of the cruelty shown them.

So ultimately what we must confront is a faith question: shall we depend on the Lord even when all the props have been pulled out from under us, like Job – in fact, like all of those mentioned above who simply threw themselves upon the Lord?

Sometimes there are clues. We may rub shoulders with people whom we might never have met otherwise, and who in a very wonderful way can demonstrate the power of the God Who is found even in the most horrible of conditions (as in the death camps). As Joseph does to Potipher [Genesis 39:2-5] and the jailer [Genesis 39:21-23], indeed we also may bring blessings to others through what seems a most unlikely environment. Or it may identify the steadfastness of God as with Jeremiah when he lives out the Lord's purpose in troubled times, even when the task of making his hearers clarify their standing in regard to God's will is most unpleasant, especially when their response breaks his heart.

Both Sts Paul and Peter call upon slaves – and us – to reframe the conditions of our circumstances:

> Whatever you do, work from your soul, as to the Lord and not for men, knowing that from the Lord you will receive the reward of [His] inheritance – you serve the Lord Christ!
> Colossians 3:23-24, also Ephesians 6:5-7

> Servants being subject to [your] masters with all respect, not only to the good and fair but also to the perverse – for this is a gift/grace if for the sake of conscience toward God, he endures pain while suffering unjustly.
> I Peter 2:18-19

What is happening is not sugar-coated, but we are called on to recognize how our Lord is active and involved in our situation, upon which we can depend. He knows our disappointments, frustrations, helplessnesses and the rest, because these same things He also experienced when He walked this earth. He is not just Overseer, He is Participant in our lives.

Therein lies our hope which "does not disappoint us, because God's love has been poured into our hearts" [Romans 5:5] – the hope in which we contemplate a powerful Love vividly displayed on the Cross and the Resurrection; in addition to the presence of the Holy Spirit Who has been given to us "as a Guarantee" [II Corinthians 1:22; 5:5; Ephesians 1:14]. This hope allows us to put one foot in front of the other, even when the environment is repugnant.

As it can be a problem of faith, it can also be a problem of attitude when it is a situation which we hate, as Betsy had to remind Corrie in regard to the fleas. Our reluctance or even defiance can bring upon ourselves additional suffering. Some grounds for refusal may have a legitimate basis, for instance, on moral or ethical grounds – or it may also be simply the rebellion in our human nature that needs to be confessed and its influence to be denied.

Our faith is challenged whether we are a Jeremiah or a Joseph. Yet in the midst of all circumstances, the Lord is also bringing His plans and goals to completion – for the sake of our lives, for other people's lives, and for the world – all based upon a Love which would save us and would value our partnership as He reveals Himself to the *cosmos*.

Just as the saints of old experience in their lives.

8. More of the Mosaic

Sources

Satan

Much in the discussion so far has identified that a great source of suffering comes through the hand of fellow humans who can be quite creative on their own. Yet we come back to the awareness of another great power with which to reckon, the power of evil particularly as centered in the Devil – "de evil one." This is one whom we must respect:

> Especially those who walk according to the flesh, in the pollution of lust and despising authority, boldly and arrogantly they do not tremble at speaking abusively of the dazzling ones[66]; whereas angels, although greater in strength and power, do not bring an abusive judgment against them before the Lord.   II Peter 2:10-11; see Jude 9-10

A useful example for our caution begins in Daniel 10, where Daniel seeks to understand a vision and so embarks upon fasting and prayer. After three weeks, suddenly he is met by an angel [vv 5-6], but notice that although his companions do not see this vision, they flee terrified from the force of its presence [v 7], and even the prophet is overwhelmed [vv 8-9]. The angel reveals that

> ... for from the first day that you set your heart to understand and to humble yourself before your God, your words were heard, and I have come because of your words. The prince of the kingdom of Persia stood against me twenty-one days; but, behold, Michael, one of the chief princes, came to help me, and I left him there with this 'king' of Persia.
> vv 12-13

As powerful as this angel seems, he is immobilized by "the prince of Persia" – who is obviously no human (since humans run from the angel's presence) – and the archangel Michael has to come to release this angel. If we then page over to Ephesians,

In Ephesians 6:12 (particularly in the King James or the Revised Standard versions), four levels of *unholy* angels are identified, the first of which are 'principalities' (see the four levels at the other end in Ephesians 1:20-23; compare with Colossians 2:10). What is reassured us, despite how powerful these four levels may seem, is that God will always be the Creator of all things – nothing is more powerful than He [Colossians 1:16].

Just what is Satan capable of doing? II Thessalonians 2:9-10, Matthew 24:24, Revelation 13:13; 16:14 describe extraordinary, very convincing, very powerful deceptions. Still they are only deceptions none the less.

That the Egyptian magicians could duplicate certain miracles done by Moses and Aaron [Exodus 7:8-12,22; 8:7] is an essential awareness, because it shows that Satan is indeed powerful and therefore not to be treated foolishly. On the other hand, note that the magicians could not stop what the Lord started [Exodus 7:24; 8:8; 9:11].

Satan gives powers, counterfeits to God's gifts, to those who will receive them without question, to those who want the power without the attachment to God. The source of 'psychic' abilities, of which our culture is so fascinated, is identified in Acts 16:16-18, where the girl is able to 'tell fortunes' with aid of a spirit not of God, which is cast out in Jesus' Name.

It is necessary to point out that this "spirit of divination" speaks accurately [verse 17]. Even though Satan is "a liar and the father of lies" [John 8:44], it is not that he cannot tell the truth when it suits him. To make deception work, it must have enough truth to sound convincing.

Nor is Satan ignorant of the future, but how much of the future he knows is only as given to him by God. The odd prophecy may be correct, but only prophets from the Lord can have the 100% accuracy that the Bible sets for itself [Deuteronomy 18:21-22, 20]. On the other hand God has harsh condemnation for 'fortune-telling' [Ezekiel 13:6-7].

Satan can make himself appear attractive enough to touch our deepest curiosities, yearnings, and even fears ("through fear of death were subject to lifelong bondage" – Hebrews 2:15). Note St Paul's warning in II Corinthians 11:13-14, how Satan can even transform himself into an angel of light – perhaps quite appropriate for our day and age.   James Lindemann[67]

This is of distinct significance as we look at suffering especially among Jehovah's People, in the Old Testament and the New. The devil is no figure in a red union suit with a tail and pitchfork, nor is he one who can be out-fiddled or out-orated.[68] He is not some benign mere influence sitting on one shoulder, while an angel on the other. He is a powerful being who has deep hatred for God and for anything which is His, along with the audacity and malice to tempt the Son of God Himself:

> We cannot attribute to Evil any sense of caring about us, any sense of merely misplaced affections – there is only raw hatred. *Any* supposed advantage *to us* is merely the lure with the hook. ... And although [Satan's temptation of Jesus] was with the *supposedly innocent purpose* of 'helping Jesus along', the real intent was to destroy Him, thereby also destroying mankind's salvation. Satan would truly get 'two birds with one stone.' The murderer has not changed from Genesis 3:4-5.
>
> James Lindemann[69]

The book of Job gives us insight in regard to the ease and swiftness by which Satan can bring about tragedy and wars; the book of Revelation reveals an extraordinary effort to murder God's Creation, namely humans, especially the saints, particularly in the last days.

He does not seek mistakes, he wants rebellion. His lies often are not so much falsehoods as much as suggestions that things *could be different*, with just enough vagueness which entices *us* to automatically "fill in the blanks" with the "obvious" ideal benefits – only to have the agony when things go sour, that it is *we* who have deluded ourselves, there is no one else to blame since we were the fools to clutch at the false picture of our own painting.

Then even after we have repented and been assured of God's forgiveness in which He "remembers the sin no more"[Jeremiah 31:34; Isaiah 43:25; Hebrews 8:12], Satan keeps resurrecting these sins, making us squirm, making us agonize, making us suffer, using the God-created ability of memory to vividly replay the embarrassments and the cruelties.

Satan wants to discourage, to manipulate, and ultimately to kill. His desire is to get us so wrapped up with fear and self-loathing that we are spiritually afraid to move lest we botch the action – all our energy is spent in introspection and in beating ourselves over the head for past (or present or future) sins real or imagined. If he cannot win us, he will do his best to so tie us up so as to make us no threat to himself.

We squelch these memories and thoughts by reminding ourselves *and Satan* that the Cross and the Resurrection have finished these sins, and if God no longer remembers them, then why are we wasting our time this way?

Satan cannot shake himself loose of his dependency on the Lord, as is evident with Job, yet still Peter warns us:

> Be sober, be vigilant; your adversary the devil walks about as a roaring lion, seeking what he may devour. Resist him, solid in the faith, knowing that the same sufferings are being experienced by your brethren in the world. I Peter 5:8-9

Despite the power and the malice behind what Satan does, our rebellion cannot be trivialized as in blaming "the Devil made me do it!" or that "I could not help myself, I am the victim!" (often an excuse for addictions). Satan wants us to believe that sin is inevitable, so that in despair we should give up even trying to not fall. Truly we will not perfectly thwart his devices, yet as Jesus dealt with his temptations by holding on to the Word of God, we have in the power of the Holy Spirit the ability to defeat Satan and to be protected from the mental anguish he seeks to press upon us.

The World

With all sorts of moral concessions being constantly emphasized in the media and culture around us, from abortions to the dismantling of marriage, from irresponsibility in the workplace to the smorgasbord of popular "spirituality," from the self-centered use of money to the discarding of the community of believers, we often end up perplexed, confused about what we are doing and should do in all kinds of settings and relationships. For those who want to "bring every thought into captivity to the obedience of Christ" [II Corinthians 10:5], opinions and criticisms from every side are introduced to emphasize the futility of such effort. A lot of what was stable in the past now appears to be shattered driftwood on the sea, and we have no confidence as to which we are to cling.

Obviously one can see the hand of Satan in this, destroying whatever he can of the Lord's design for humanity and the universe, and yet we should not assign to people the role of innocent victim in all this. Isaiah's "We have turned, every one, to his own way" [53:6] reminds us that sometimes we are not even following Satan's plans when we embark on some sin. Was Pilate's wife's message to him when Jesus was about to be condemned, "Let there be nothing between you and that righteous man – I have suffered many things today in a dream because of him!" [Matthew 27:19] the attempt of Satan to put on the brakes to what the humans were now running on to on their own, possibly because the Devil began to realize the effect of Jesus' death on him? Of course, on the other hand it could be simply the Devil making sure that Pilate knew what was wrong before it did it, as the Serpent made sure that Eve states the Creator's prohibition in regard to the forbidden fruit [Genesis 3:1-3], so that Pilate was fully aware that he was rebelling against even his own standards.

"The Fifth Column"

A squeal of tires and a sickening thud heralded to two young boys the death of their pet cat. Although they felt sad, they were also fascinated by their first exposure to death. At first they were just going to leave the cat, to watch what would happen to it, but their parents were firm that it was to be buried. Reluctantly they obeyed, but then hit upon an idea. they would indeed bury it, but would leave the tail sticking out. The next day, they pulled on the tail to check on their friend, and then covered it again with the tail left out. After a couple of days, when the parents discovered their plan, it was insisted the cat be fully buried *tail and all.*

When Napoleon came to take Paris with four armies, there were so many sympathizers in the city that he called them his "fifth column.." The problem humanity faces is that Satan and this world have an ally – a "fifth column" – in our human nature, or "the flesh," which, like the young boys, is fascinated by that which destroys life and relationships.

> Because all which is in the world – the lust of the flesh, the lust of the eyes, and the arrogance of earthly life – is not of the Father but is of the world.   I John 2:16

> But now you put off all these things: anger, rage, malice, abuse, filthy language out of your mouth.   Colossians 3:8

> For the past time was enough to have worked the Gentile will – when we walked in wantonness, lusts, drunkenness, carousing, drinking parties, and lawless idolatries.   I Peter 4:3

Human nature is enthralled by what ultimately is spiritually putrid: inspecting it, handling it, playing with it, covering oneself with it. In an eerie way, it is like the current fascination with zombies, where people even will use make-up and dress like them, walk like them and otherwise try to mimic the way such "living dead" would be, rather than to emphasize the joy and exhilaration of life. "The flesh"'s fascination with the direct opposite of God's Life and purpose for us on this earth is fertile ground for temptation. Even seeing a list as in the above Bible passages, or to hear of anything forbidden, often raises a strong attraction:

... I would not have known sin if not by the Law: indeed, I would not be aware of covetousness if the Law had never said, "You shall not covet." But sin, having taken the opportunity through the commandment, produced in me all kinds of covetousness. For apart from the Law sin was dead, ... The commandment, which should bring life, was found to be death to me. For sin, taking occasion by the commandment, deceived me, and murdered me.   Romans 7:7-11

Or as St James put it:

But every one is tempted – lured and baited by his own desires; then desire, having conceived, gives birth to sin; and sin, having matured, brings forth death.   James 1:14-15

All humans experience the digging in of temptation's claws, although believers will most feel its stinging grip, because their concern is to please their Lord, therefore the moral threshold is higher and the distance to human nature's desires is the more pronounced. Temptation is indeed tenacious, often like a nagging child, simply repeating its desires over and over until we simply are worn down. It seems that the harder we struggle against it, the more powerful it grows because actually we become so focused on denying the sin that it simply fills our field of vision and we see nothing else. Consequently it becomes overwhelming.

Although not so much a physical suffering, the mental and spiritual struggle can be very exhausting, creating emotional anguish between doing right or following human nature's gratification, as nights become restless and days slip preoccupied away. The answer to such temptation is surprisingly simple – (although it doers take training and practice) just stop fighting, that is, stop focusing on the temptation and instead turn the mind to Someone else, as Jesus did for His temptations [Matthew 4 and Luke 4].

You have put off the Old (according to your former behavior) Man, which is corrupt through deceitful lusts, now be renewed in the spirit of your mind – you have put on the New Man, created in true righteousness and holiness which reflects God..   Ephesians 4:22-24

But now *you,* put off all these things: anger, rage, malice, abuse, filthy language out of your mouth! Do not lie to one another, having put off the old man with its practices; you have put on the new nature which is being renewed in knowledge according to the image of its Creator.

Colossians 3:7-10

It is simple! However, we are not really talking about its simplicity, despite how this solution can and does work: the actual problem is that our human nature is unwilling to let the temptation go, whether it be worry, lust, pride, or whatever it may be. It is not just a matter of handling this or that temptation:

> There is a difference though between the *root* of the temptation and the *symptoms* of the temptation. The problem in dealing with just the symptoms (such as with "fornication, impurity, licentiousness, idolatry, sorcery, enmity, strife, jealousy, anger, selfishness, dissension, divisiveness, envy, drunkenness, carousing, and the like" [Galatians 5:19-21]) is that the root keeps producing fruit, or else it erupts elsewhere in a different way. Jesus identified the root: "For from within, out of the heart of man, come evil thoughts, fornication, … All these evil things come from within, and they defile a man" [Mark 7:21-23].
>
> James Lindemann[70]

Just like faith in the Lord has to come because of the outside influence of the Holy Spirit, so also He must step in here to make us release our grasp on a sin. His Ally, of course, is the outstanding experienced help in Jesus Himself: "For in that He Himself has suffered, being tempted, He is able to aid those who are tempted" [Hebrews 2:18]. The good news is that the Holy Spirit does not give up, and does release our grasp on sin, although sometimes one finger at a time, slowly but surely giving us real progress. He not only addresses the temptation, but also the root of the problem, changing our heart, attitudes, values, perspectives and so much more.

Nature

Is all suffering initiated solely from Satan? Admittedly Satan is eager to have his hand in whatever distress we may have, yet Isaiah indicates humans can also come up with effective rebellions on our own: "All we like sheep have gone astray; each of us has turned to his own path" [Isaiah 53:6]. There is another source identified in Genesis 3:17-18, the ground is cursed and now resists humanity's efforts to manage it, the indication being that some suffering comes simply from nature itself. Romans tells us that "creation was subjected to futility ... the bondage of corruption" [8:20-21] which describes a universe deteriorating on its own, not necessarily by the Devil's initiative.

The raw power of nature, Proverbs 8:24-31 tells us, is held in check by God – He establishes its boundaries, to tell it where it can go and no further. In the Pincher Creek, Alberta flood of 1995, after eleven inches of rain in twelve hours, we stood almost disbelieving the tremendous power of the water, yet also realizing our utter helplessness to stop it, much less if anyone fell in, to survive it. In literally one day, how easily we were simply overwhelmed, and that everything we had built, worked for, saved, enjoyed, and cherished could simply be swept away – all because just for a moment, God "took His hands off the steering wheel" and removed the boundaries to only one of the awful destructive forces all around us.

Why does God sometimes allow nature to go unbridled? All we can do is make guesses, and perhaps some would indeed be what God intended. Possibly it is His shock treatment to make us realize just what is ultimately important in our lives, to get us to evaluate whether we have fallen into "majoring in the minors" in regard to the *things* of our lives rather than His will and design for humanity.

But perhaps it is also to remind us – who can do all sorts of things that virtually make us seem like gods, seem like we are in control of our destiny, seem like we have a handle on our world – that all it takes is one day to radically change all that. Like earthquake victims who no longer have confidence in good old "Terra Firma," one becomes just a little more cautious about the weather and the "creek."

However, again "the buck stops here" at the throne of God. Realizing that there are all sorts of forces out there which could so easily "do us in," it is comforting to know that the Creator does hold them in check – but even more comforting is His reason why: He "rejoices in creation and delights in mankind" [Proverbs 8:31]. We have become aware of what nature unrestrained can be like, yet, never out of God's control, it is merely just one more thread in the tapestry of our lives.

Choosing to Suffer

It is useful to see the contrast: often we see ourselves as victims of suffering, but there is a side in which suffering is deliberately chosen.

Selfishness and Altruism

This writer had a discussion once in which the other person defined human activity from the viewpoint promoted by Ayn Rand, where she declared that everything is basically done because of selfishness, that the only reason why someone does anything is because of its expected benefit to himself. Because of fallen human nature, it is hard to refute that argument, since the rebellion of sin, especially its selfishness, salts everything we do. St Paul talks about that in Romans 7, and CS Lewis describes above how much self-pride plays its role in one out of every three or so thoughts.

Yet are there not times when true altruism raises its head? The ultimate example is found in Jesus' words: "Greater Love has no one than this, that a man lay down his Life for his friends" [John 15:13]. There are many examples of people who step up to give their lives for others. One may think of "the first responders" – police, firemen, medical people – who "run toward what everyone else is running from," and as we saw in the fall of the New York City World Trade towers, many gave their lives. If we were stuck in a burning building, we would deeply appreciate the firemen who risk their lives to save us, whereas the philosophy of selfishness would demand that they are fools to do so do so and we should be left to die. So also one would expect in such a framework that a parent should not sacrifice in any way for the child, but should leave the child at the mercy of whatever threatens its life and wellbeing.

Selfishness was described as, "whatever good they might do, they do it because of the good feeling and sense of self-worth they get," yet if they die, that really becomes a very hollow reason. In especially Ernest Gordon's account of the Japanese death camps, to save their comrades – so that many would not needlessly die –, some step forward to experience the full hatred of their captors. Yes, perhaps there is the thought that after their death others might remember them – if those prisoners survive at all – , but when you are dead, *you* will not reap that benefit.

Well, at least for believers (although selfishness has no interest in acknowledging a God), should they somehow give their lives for someone else, it would only mean that they hope to receive a reward for their selfish self-sacrifice. Somehow, though, it seems strange to think of the Judge of all the earth saying so someone, "You have been *so* selfish, that you deserve a big reward!" Instead, what impresses the people in the camps is how unselfish are those who do not try to make themselves survive by the brushing others aside. And it is precisely this which makes the prisoners examine anew their discarded faith. As well, what we find so "heroic" about first responders is not their selfishness, but rather their willingness to give up everything they hold dear, even their lives if need be, to give others life, even to complete strangers. In other words, it is not self*ish*ness which breathes life into an atmosphere of death, but rather self*less*ness.

Ironically even God gets tagged with an interpretation of selfishness, as when He is described as basically being lonely and that the reason why He would create mankind is in order to have someone to love Him in return. Easily what happens is as St Paul put it: "All things are pure to the pure, but to the corrupt and disbelieving nothing is pure; rather they are corrupted in both the mind and the conscience" [Titus 1:15] – in our fallen human nature, it is hard to see love as a creative self-giving rather than merely the setting up of a selfish environment.

Understanding Altruism

… focusing on the Author and Completer of our faith, Jesus, Who for the joy lying before Him endured the Cross, having despised the shame, and now sits at the right hand of the throne of God   Hebrews 12:2

How then should we understand this passage? Would joy be a selfish motive? Not like what is being talked about above. The potential of joy for a first responder in saving a life is only a by-product of that which may not happen in many rescues. Even when there is no hope for a successful rescue, the first responder still often risks his life to follow his commitment. In other words, many times he will do his vocation (calling), even when there is no prospect for self-benefit, other than the satisfaction that he has done what he could.

138

Some might interpret "the joy" as selfishness in regard to Jesus, until John declares in both his Gospel and his first letter that the Lord dies for the whole world. Over the course of humanity, how many countless times has His rescue been rejected? Having a failure is not a joyful thing – there is no self-benefit, so selfishness would withdraw its commitment to only those believers where He would get His satisfaction. We discover that the opposite is the case: He continues to bear the sins of *all* mankind. *Every* sin pulls Him down against the nails and turns the sky black in His forsakenness. He will not discriminate in His Love.

And turn it around: suppose only one person was a sinner, would Jesus have died for only one? Is this really so hard to understand? Would a first responder risk his life if only one person needed rescuing? The parable of the one lost sheep out of a flock of a hundred [Matthew 18:12; Luke 15:4] indicates the value of one – *even if the one refuses to be rescued.* Selfishness is a nice and comfortable way of isolating oneself from the difficulties of the world, but when we need help in extreme circumstances, the fortress of selfishness begins to crumble as we hope that others will not have the same philosophy.

When Love Runs Toward Suffering

> … indeed God's heirs and joint-heirs with Christ, provided we jointly suffer in order that we may also be jointly glorified. For I conclude that the sufferings of this present time are not worthy in light of the Glory about to be revealed in us.   Romans 8:17-18

Mine unions were first formed because the situation was a virtual slavery for the men and their families while the owners had disregard for the safety of their workers. The initial strikes were met with much violence between the owners' created "goon squads" and the strikers determination to not let strike-breakers destroy their efforts. Still the miners realized that the picture was much larger and that they had chosen a path of suffering in which perhaps they might never survive nor benefit, however, at least others would have better working and living conditions.

Christianity has been described as a former starving beggar telling a still starving beggar where to find bread. The early Christians were committed to not selfishness but to doing what they could to let others know that there was freedom and life to be had. It is curious how hard humanity will fight against having this news shared, but the believers were determined to be God's People to their culture. They did not fight back except with God's Love; they realized that they had chosen suffering and possibly martyrdom to bring a new order into the world, where others would reap the benefits of what they had sown. Sts Peter and Paul sets the perspective:

> They therefore departed from the presence of the council, rejoicing that they were counted worthy to be dishonored on account of His Name.
> Acts 5:41

> Having laid many blows upon them, they cast them into prison, charging the jailer to keep them securely. Having received such a charge, he threw them into the inner prison and fastened their feet in the stocks. Toward midnight Paul and Silas were praying and singing hymns to God while the prisoners were listening to them. Acts 16:23-25

This does not mean that opportunities to escape injustice should be discarded in a distorted desire for self-admiration, but rather to understand that in many circumstances such options may be discarded because the goal set before us, as was set before Jesus, is just too valuable – the ability to give Life is just too precious.

The Great Exchange

As Jesus stood before Pilate, both Mark and Luke, and even John's "robber" (possibility meaning "insurrectionist"), identify Barabbas as what we would call a "terrorist" [Matthew 27:16-26; Mark 15:6-15; Luke 23:17-25;

140

John 18:40], possibly one of that day's "*sicarii*" or "Zealot" groups. As often throughout history, such efforts to "free the people" from "oppression" have death, destruction and a new tyranny as their companions.

On the other hand is Jesus, Who desires that a person be released from sin, its power and its effects, as well as that he be given a new worth in sonship to God Himself. The Lord is declared absolutely innocent by Pilate [Luke 23:4; John 19:4] and other sources [Isaiah 53:9; II Corinthians 5:21; I Peter 2:22; I John 3:5]); in fact, false witnesses could not make even a *false* accusation stick [Matthew 26:59-63; Mark 14:56-59].

The stage is set for a most amazing exchange: Barabbas is released, while Jesus is condemned – the innocent dies the agonized death, while the guilty lives in full freedom. But this is no mere objectionable miscarriage of justice, rather Jesus deliberately takes upon Himself the penalty, the suffering, and the death that the rebellious deserve; meanwhile the very humans who have caused so much of the misery and suffering in the world are offered everything which His innocence deserves. It certainly is not *fair*, yet Jesus voluntarily shoulders the full weight of the guilt.

It is the expression of the intense wish a family experiences when they stand at the bedside of a suffering or dying loved one, the wish that they could take some of the pain, or give some of their strength to that one. *Their* private agony is their helplessness, but what happens *there* symbolically is what Jesus does ultimately: He does take the pain which we will never know, while giving us the strength of His relationship with His Father – this is a most unique twist in our discussion on suffering!

The "kicker" comes in the meaning of the name "Barabbas": "The Father's Son." There are two "Father's Son"s here – Barabbas and Jesus. For Barabbas, the name has been merely a label; for Jesus, it is a description of His Divine nature. Taking upon Himself the deserved suffering of

Barabbas, Jesus offers in return to fill this man's name with real meaning – giving him "the right to become children of God, to those who believe in His Name" [John 1.12]

Barabbas is never mentioned again. How he responds to this exchange of life and death, freedom and suffering, there is no indication. We are left hanging, probably deliberately so because there is a *third* Barabbas: in Baptism, "Behold what sort of Love the Father has bestowed upon us, that we should be called children of God – and we are!" [I John 3:1] – Barabbas' story has been precisely *our* story as well! We are pulled into the Biblical account to write our own completion, whether it be good or bad, whether "Barabbas" remains merely a label or, in Jesus, it becomes fact.

God's Chosen Suffering to End Suffering

When Paul links suffering to "hope" in Romans 5:1-5, it is a hope which "does not disappoint us" despite the suffering and endurance which has been required. Within the vastness of the universe; Psalm 8 marks the wonder of "when I see Your heavens, the work of Your fingers, … what is man that You remember him, and the son of man that You visit him?" [v 3-4].

In answer, the Bible is the record and the Cross is the evidence that God does care, that He does delight in humanity – and the Resurrection affirms that there is a destination designed for believers, who are themselves designed for that destination at His side, on His throne. Here is a hope grounded in the reality of a Love from God which does not hesitate nor stumble at giving each believer literally everything He is, a Love which is *poured* into our hearts through the Holy Spirit.

It is a hope and Love which addresses spiritual suffering, but through the hands of fellow believers also touches physical suffering. As with the inmates of the death camps, the surrounding circumstances may not be

142

changed, but there is strength and courage, care and nurturing, fellowship and understanding [Philippians 2:1-2], through which even physical suffering can become more tolerable, all with the confident concrete anticipation that one day:

> God will wipe away every tear from their eyes; death shall be no more, nor grief, nor crying, nor pain any longer, for the former things have passed away. Revelation 21:4

Just Plain Grit

How eagerly we would desire that all this suffering is finished. How we wish we were included in the information loop in regard to our circumstances, so that knowing the plan, we can know in which direction to go, and how to handle the next situation. Job would understand. Growing in patience has its own kind of suffering, and it is struggle with faith.

> Though it is true that he questions God's fairness and goodness and love, and despairs of his own life, Job refuses to turn his back on God. "Though he slay me, yet will I hope in him," he defiantly insists (13:15). He may have given up on God's justice, but he stubbornly refuses to give up on God. At the most unlikely moments of despair, he comes up with brilliant flashes of hope and faith (9:33; 16:19-21). Philip Yancey[71]

9. The Last Chapter, Not the Last Word

A Continuing Story

> Though He was a Son, by the things which He suffered He learned obedience. Having been brought to completion, He became *the Author of eternal salvation* to all who obey Him … focusing on *the Author and Completer of our faith, Jesus,* Who for the joy lying before Him endured the Cross, having despised the shame, and now sits at the right hand of the Throne of God   Hebrews 5:8-9; 12:2

A writer once remarked at how the above passages are favorites of hers, since her fellow Master Author is still in the process of writing "her book" (her life), and although she knows the ending already ("eternal salvation"), she is eager to see *how* it will be finished and what will be written for today.

Although this book is ending, the discussion on suffering includes far too much to fit in any book, and even our own "story" (for most of us) is not yet in its final chapter. At times our "story" has appeared to have a "writer's block" – seemingly going nowhere –, yet in looking back, we find in each day's page the plot has continued to be developed, each day the storyline has moved closer to its completion. The Author has never and will never abandon the project, nor will He "suffer" from a lack of content for each day.

The odd thing about such a "book" is that it is a collaborative effort between the Master Author and His main character. The stakes are high – after all, as Job and other have shown, we simply do not know who all will be "reading" the account, waiting for the next page to be penned out; and we also must wait for our page of today, ignorant of where the plot is going. But the most amazing aspect is that just like with Job, God allows us to influence the day's work – we can affect the story of our lives by our own choices.

Even more so, not only do our choices have impact, such as when Job chooses to not "curse God and die" or when St Peter in his first letter encourages us to do good even when it is criticized and misinterpreted [I, 3:15-16], we can ask *the Author* Himself to change the daily narrative by doing or giving something:

> Again I say to you truly, that if two of you agree concerning any matter on the earth, that if they ask, it will be done to them by My Father Who is in heaven. Matthew 18:19

> Whatever you have asked in My Name, this I will do, so that the Father may be glorified in the Son. If you ask anything in My Name, I will do it. John 14:13-14

What is His aspiration behind all this?

> For I know the plans that I have designed for you," says Jehovah, "plans of peace and not of evil, to give you a future and a hope. Then you will call upon Me and come and pray to Me, and I will listen to you. You will seek Me and find Me; when you search for Me with all your heart, I will be found by you," says Jehovah. …
> Thus says Jehovah Who made it, Jehovah Who formed it to establish it – Jehovah is His Name: Call to Me and I will answer you, and will disclose to you great and impenetratable things which you did not know. Jeremiah 29:11-14; 33:2-3

Indeed the "book" of our lives has an astonishing collaboration! Still, as we have seen, the Author maintains the Editor's privilege to "adjust" the material so that it ultimately achieves His heartfelt desire for what our life can be and how it will arrive at His climatic event (the Last Day) which sets the base for His eternal sequel.

Confidence

For this cause I also suffer these things; but I am not ashamed, *for I know Whom I have believed* and I am persuaded that He is able to watch over what I have entrusted to Him until that Day.   II Timothy 1:12

As the above Hebrews verses point out, our story is not just of actions and events, it is also more specifically about our faith and the "finishing" touches which the Author Himself brings to this relationship. He knows very well the territory of human life and how suffering can bring out contrasts and highlights within our personal histories.

Yet what guarantee do we have whether His predisposition toward us is for good or for evil? In reply is Paul's pivotal claim in his letter to Timothy: *"for I know Whom I have believed"*! It is not just we who are placed under the microscope, God has also put Himself where He can be closely examined, where we can look into His heart and into His very root motives for us – the most profound example being Jesus, where St John recounts:

> That Which was from the beginning, Which we have *heard*, Which we have *seen* with our eyes, Which we have *looked upon*, and our hands have *handled*, concerning the Word of Life – the Life was *manifested*, and we have *seen*, and bear witness, and proclaim to you that Life Eternal which was with the Father and was manifested to us – that Which we have *seen* and *heard* we declare to you, that you also may have fellowship [participation] with us; and indeed our fellowship [participation] is with the Father and with His Son Jesus Christ. These things we write to you that your joy may be full.   I John 1:1-4

This is why Paul can be so confident: there is concrete evidence, physical evidence, evidence that could actually be handled and observed. Even if he is not clear as to the whys or any other details of what happens in his life, at least he knows with Whom he is dealing. He knows the Cross and the motivation behind it, he knows the Presence and the resources, especially *the* Resource, the Holy Spirit, and the other resources to be found in God's People, the Church. He has held God's diary, the Scriptures, up to the glare of the sun and found that it speaks wonderful truth.

He has the same confidence which Job confesses, who, despite the absolute confusion as to what God is doing at the moment, can still declare his belief that the ultimate outcome will be for him to personally stand in the Lord's presence on the Last Day [Job 23-27].

It is a confidence which also comes because the Holy Spirit has made His home in our hearts, and this is a basis of the power to face whatever Satan, the world, and even our human nature, can throw at us:

> You are of God, little children, and have overcome them, because greater is He Who is in you than he who is in the world. ... For all who have been born of God overcome the world; and this is the victory which has overcome the world – our faith. Who is he who overcomes the world, if not he who believes that Jesus is the Son of God?   I John 4:4; 5:4-5

It is an assurance that we can depend on because its foundation is on a solid Rock.

Love

In the midst of suffering, Paul is convinced of God's Love as we also must be. Do not skip too lightly over the Cross – that suffering which has been chosen, that suffering which is caused by rebellion, that suffering which *we* cause –, it is much too essential to the story.

From the very beginning the Creator has fully understood what it would cost – cost Him as well as the humanity He creates – when He gives humans the ability to choose to not love. By doing so, He signs the death warrant for His own Son. And yet that Son willingly comes. He knows what will await Him. He knows ... when at twelve years old He is ready to be "about His Father's business." He knows ... as He passes those who are crucified

148

(since the Romans always crucified on the major thoroughfares into a city), hearing their cries, their moans, their suffering every year of His life; He knows … that one day He will be on one of those crosses. Yet He bows His head and becomes "obedient unto death" [Philippians 2:8].

Consider the Love which compels Jesus' every dragged step up that hill of Golgatha, note also in Gethsemane the revulsion He feels toward what He faces. Yet He is determined to see His Love through. His choice is not easy. If it were us instead of Jesus, how long would it be before we "pull up stakes and go home"? How well Satan knows his Target in his temptations of our Lord, offering Him the easy way to be "the Lord," "the King" and "the Messiah," rather than this route to the Cross!

As we follow the progression of His suffering, we are struck by how easily Jesus could have bailed out at any time [Matthew 26:53; John 18:36], but He refuses. In fact, time and again He equips His captors to fulfill their intent [John 18:3-9; Luke 22:50-51; Matthew 26:60-66; 27:11-14]. In other words, the permission to crucify Him comes not so much from the Father, as it comes from Jesus Himself, which is in contrast to what we had just seen in Gethsemane. This is why the Cross is the definition of Love, not only of the Father's Love in sending His Son, but also in Jesus' choice to die – but then to rise from the dead.

Although the Creator has given humans the ability to choose not to love, for Him there is no such choice. He has to love, He is love. And He will choose the suffering. He will be personally involved and do what nothing else in the universe could do in His place. He Himself will experience the suffering which humans have brought on themselves, He will come to carry the burden of all of their sins, He will pay the death that the Law demands of every single human being – for every single one of us. He will reach out to the victims of sin, of death, of Satan; not in a bland, over-the-shoulder "whoever ... whatever ...," the description of indifference, but rather in the "whoever" of John 3:14-16 where every individual is noticed and invited. He will do this out of love.

There is power here to face and handle tragedies. There is power here which includes greater than just this world, a power which wraps its arms around eternity. There is power here which tells us that God stands with us no matter what the circumstances may be. There is power here in which God does not insulate even Himself from the realities that surround us even now.

This is the rock solid foundation for Paul's absolute confidence – he knows in Whom he believes and therefore "I am not ashamed of the Gospel, for it is the *power [dynamite] of God* into salvation, to everyone who believes" [Romans 1:16].

Father!

Yet the Holy Spirit does not give up – by means of events in their lives, by troubles and difficulties, by some so-called chance word, by some so-called chance visit to a church, by some word of God or testimony He calls men and women back to Himself.

I heard a wonderful illustration of this only last week. A pastor was called to New Haven for a Baptism. He explained Baptism to the assembled group. Afterwards a man came up and asked for a few words alone. He said that several months before he and his wife had received the news that she had cancer and was not expected to live but a short while. When they finally understood this, his wife turned to him and said: "It's been a long time since we have prayed, let's pray." But what should they pray? It had been so long they had forgotten how. They knelt down and tried to pray the Our Father. They started strongly, but the first few petitions made them stumble. They had no copy of it, and so they had to struggle through, going over and over again until they had what they thought was the Our Father. The man said that he rose from that prayer as he had never experienced anything before – a flowing of strength, for they had decided not to pray that she be spared or healed, but only that they might have the strength to face the coming days. Suddenly he found himself bursting forth with one word, he spoke it:

"Father!" He had learned something new – God was his Father and had finally realized it – and in a sense of wonder he repeated it many times through those days. His wife died, but that was incidental to their joyous discovery that the Father's Love was greater than their love for each other, greater than terminal disease, and they were swallowed up in His love. Robert F Lindemann[72]

What an astonishing asset to have in the midst of suffering, to be placed into this most extraordinary of relationships, to be beloved children of God Himself [John 1:12-13], and it is so simple!

Told he must be born of water and the Spirit, bewildered, Nicodemus asks how this can be? Jesus directs attention to the Serpent in the wilderness: "As Moses lifted up the serpent in the wilderness, even so must the Son of Man be lifted up, so that whoever believes in Him should not perish but have eternal life" [John 3:14-15].

Israel had rebelled in their wilderness journey and fiery serpents with deadly bites were sent among them [Numbers 21]. As they cried to the Lord, Moses was instructed to make a bronze model of a serpent and put it on a high pole in the center of the camp. Then, "when anyone is bitten, when he sees the [the snake Moses made], he shall live" [v 8]. It had nothing to do with one's accomplishments – to survive, it must be done God's way, the way of faith.

It was easy – one simply had to look to be saved. He didn't have to identify its shape, count its scales – he didn't even have to see it clearly: it may have been only a glint in the distance, but that was all he needed, because he was doing it God's way. It did not matter if he were a well-educated priest, or an unlettered slave – all that he had to know was that salvation was found in the promise attached to that symbol on the pole, not by spiritual gymnastics, nor by a code of laws, nor by an accumulation of knowledge, nor by age nor gender, but by simply looking to the promise.[73]

So also is becoming the child of God attached to the promise found in Jesus, the Man Who is also God, Who was lifted up on a Cross. Why so simple? Jesus continues to Nicodemus. "For God so loved the world that He gave His only Son," and again, "so that whoever believes in Him may not perish but have eternal life" [John 3:16] – both parts of His answer [vv 15,16] end with exactly the same words. We also receive by faith all that is promised simply "because God loves us that much," and the "whoever" is the indication of how encompassing is His Love for every individual. There is no way to understand this extraordinary love of God – other than it just is this way.

This is the security of God's promise and of God's love which can bring life, strength and hope into our lives, even as death comes knocking at the door as in the death camps. It is the confidence that reveals to us that we have a loving Father Who will do so much for us, even when it costs the life of His Son. It is the powerful seriousness that God has when He makes us His Children so that we know that we can come to Him boldly. It is the comfort of knowing He will listen, even to the deep things of our hearts, because His Holy Spirit makes that place, our hearts, His home. He is *still* this serious about us being His Children. Here is the confirmation that as Jesus put it, "because I live, you also shall live."

Confidence (Reprise)

What is man, that You make him so precious, that You set Your heart on him, that You attend to him in the morning, and examine him in the moment? Why will You not look away from me and let me alone till I swallow my spit? Job 7:17-19

Job is really annoyed at Jehovah's close scrutiny of him, but there is an important contrast to this passage found in Psalm 8:

what is man that You remember him, and the son of man that You visit him? You have made him a little lower than God, and have crowned him with glory and honor. vv 4-5

The first passage accents our fear and discomfort should God would get too close and see too much, that He does not just stop at the more appealing façade but goes far deeper into our lives. Even with the words, "Well, nobody's perfect," we identify how well we know that we cannot stand under the close inspection of the Lord's perceptive eye. However, there is none of that fear in the second passage. Instead there is delight and rejoicing in the companionship which the psalmist has with Him.

St Paul has expressed in the above his confidence in knowing the heart of God in Jesus, and in Romans 8, he has made the journey from the human's natural suspicion of God's personal interest in him to the psalmist's pleasure at being God's partner in Creation. The idea that the Holy Spirit has made His home in our hearts – God has come *this* close to us – has become for Paul a most wonderful asset for living. The Spirit bears witness of his Sonship to God [v 16], therefore with the Spirit living in us, now *we* are alive [v 11]; no longer subject to fear, we can approach the Father using a Name of familiarity and endearment: "Abba" or "Daddy" [v 15]; and we become joint-heirs with Jesus Himself. The Spirit's scrutiny of our hearts is not to triumphantly point the finger at our lacks and weaknesses (which our human nature suspects), rather He is to aid our limited ability to communicate, translating the deep things in our hearts, for which we can find no adequate words, into what God (the Father and the Son) can fully understand [vv 26-27]. Finally, Paul steps back in amazement at how committed God is to us – to freely give what we need [v 32] and that nothing can possibly separate us from His Love [vv 38-39].

Not only is Paul confident in the extraordinary Love of God, but he is also confident in the standing that the believer has with this God. He knows that whatever suffering may come his way, even "tribulation, or distress, or persecution, or famine, or nakedness, or peril, or sword" [v 35], that "we know that He makes all things work together for good for those who love God, for those who are called according to His purpose" [v 28]. Like Job, he may not know the whys of what he is enduring, but he understands the value of the Holy Spirit being so close and personal, and of his being under the watchful, caring, helpful and protecting eye of God Himself.

And also, like Job, it is the security of knowing that as we flail about in our agony of suffering, we also may speak too hasty and ill-advised words of despair and indignation (like Job's depiction of God as one who simply "makes an end of both the blameless and the wicked" [Job 9:22], or his challenge: "Is it pleasant to You to oppress and to cast off the work of Your hands, and to shine brightly on the schemes of the wicked?" [10:3]); yet as his Creator calls him to repentance and humility, he is forgiven. And then he is praised

> Jehovah said to Eliphaz, "My wrath is kindled at you and at your two friends because you have not spoken what is right as My servant Job has. … My servant Job shall pray for you, for I will accept him …"
>
> Job 42:7-8

What an amazing confidence we are placed into which is of great comfort even in times of suffering!

Contentment

This ability to closely inspect God's Love is what gives us our confidence, as it does to St Paul, and imagine this man's response – *his* joy, *his* choice, *his* "contentment":

> On this account, that I may not be exalted by the outstanding revelations, a thorn for the flesh was given to me, a messenger of Satan to torment me, that I might not be arrogant. Three times I begged the

154

Lord that it might be removed from me, but He said to me, "My grace is sufficient for you, for indeed power is perfected in weakness." Most gladly therefore will I rather boast in my weaknesses, that the power of Christ may dwell upon me. Therefore I am pleased in weaknesses, in insults, in dire need, in persecutions, in distresses, for Christ's sake; for when I am weak, then I am strong.   II Corinthians 12:7-10

He is surround by Love beyond measure, in the midst of frustration and humility. He discovers the wisdom of God as deep and profound and wonderful, and it is able to handle all suffering. Everything which Jesus has, especially in His Resurrection, rings out the proclamation that Paul now shares in his Lord's victory and life – just as Jesus has shared in *his* life and humanity. Jesus promised, "The Holy Spirit will take what is Mine and declare it to you" [John 16:14-15] – will "pour it into you," a hope, Paul writes, which we have because God's Love is poured into our hearts by the Holy Spirit! [Romans 5:5]. Here is to be found strength, assurance, and courage.

It is a real-world Love, suffering and all, which Paul prefers; not some insipid "love" which runs from pain and condemns as defective those who suffer.

In short, Job's friends emerge as self-righteous dogmatists who defend the mysterious ways of God. They are properly scandalized by Job's outbursts. ... A modern-day bumper sticker captures their condescending tone succinctly: "If you feel far from God, guess who moved."

Philip Yancey[74]

Paul's reply is that likely nobody moved! In fact, as Yancey remarks:

At the very moment when Job felt most abandoned, at that moment God was giving him personal, almost microscopic attention. God seemed absent to him; in one sense, God had never been more present.[75]

The Lord could not be closer or less involved: Paul also is shown that he has a never-withdrawn participation in Jehovah's work, a participation in the Creator's heart, and a participation in Jesus' suffering [Romans 8:17], reflecting this God to those around him. In the Love he experiences, which goes the farthest distance for him, he willingly responds by suffering for those outside and for those inside the grace and mercy of God. Through the Holy Spirit, he is equipped to walk with those who also suffer, with the reassurance that whatever he does, whether he sees it or not, it will never be in vain [I Corinthians 15:57-58] – he does make a far-reaching, even universe-wide difference.

> For Job, the battleground of faith involved lost possessions, lost family members, lost health. We may face a different struggle: a career failure, a floundering marriage, sexual orientation, a face or body shape that turns people off, not on. REGARDLESS, THE MESSAGE OF THIS BOOK CALLS FOR THE HARD-EDGED FAITH THAT BELIEVES, AGAINST ALL ODDS, THAT ONE PERSON'S RESPONSE OF OBEDIENCE DOES MAKE A DIFFERENCE.
>
> Philip Yancey[76]

This is a true contentment which can find its peace even in concentration camps, even in the midst of cruelty and suffering and death. In the words for which Betsy taught Corrie the meaning, there is a strong foundation in which to: "Always rejoice, unceasingly pray, in everything give thanks; for this is God's will in Christ Jesus in you" [I Thessalonians 5:16-18].

"That We May Comfort"

> Blessed be the God and Father of our Lord Jesus Christ, the Father of compassion and God of all comfort, Who comforts us in all our affliction, so that we may be able to comfort those who are in any affliction through the comfort with which we ourselves are comforted by God. Because as Christ's sufferings abound in us, so through Christ our comfort also abounds.
>
> II Corinthians 1:3-5

Many times when we have experienced a bruise, there is a new sensitivity to pain in that spot for the time being. Other suffering does the same: although on one hand it may make us focus into ourselves, on the other hand, we become more sensitive to others who may suffering especially in the same area where we have been "bruised." There is a tension since the Creator has made us be His Image to the universe and we are drawn out of ourselves to touch others in compassion. So a cancer survivor becomes more aware of other cancer sufferers and therefore can reach out in understanding and support. Sufferers of cruelty reach out with affirmation and hope to those who also feel destroyed. Sometimes it may be to give a validation that the other person is indeed progressing in their healing. Sometimes it is simply to give a person someone to whom to cling as he is confronted with a staggering and even frightening situation, as a reassurance that he is not abandoned by the Lord's representative, nor by the Lord Himself.

God's response may even be to us, "No, this is not your task – although I want you to be sensitive to this, I am calling someone else who is better equipped in these circumstances into action – I must give that person the chance to choose – and your support is for *that* person." This can sometimes be a whole different suffering of our own because of the humility and patience which this requires! There are times when like St Paul we "planted, Apollos watered, but God gave the increase" [I Corinthians 3:6].

And outcomes are not always satisfying. Allowing love, allowing choices, stepping aside for another will not be a magic cure-all, nor will results always be immediate. Nor will those results always be what we really want to see, just as there are times when we must reflect the broken heart of our Lord:

As He drew near, having seen the city, He wept over it, saying, "If you, especially you, had known today the things which are for [God's] peace! But now they are hidden from your eyes."   Luke 19:41-42

Of such is the Love and its suffering in which we participate, yet this is crucial as our Lord carries out His heart's desire to bring His life into the rebellion-tainted universe.

Prayer

In *Through the Valley of the Kwai*, the prisoners discover their situation does not change because of their prayers and other "religious" activity, and at first they throw away their faith. Job never does find out why he has to suffer. However, in II Kings 20, King Hezekiah's prayer brings not only healing, fifteen years are also added to his life. In the Gospels, those who come to Jesus are healed, yet St Paul is not relieved of his "thorn in the flesh" [II Corinthians 12:7-10]. Jesus insists, in John 14 through 16, "If you ask anything in My Name, I will do it" [14:14]; "…you will ask whatever you will and it will come to pass to you" [15:7]; "Until now you have asked for nothing in My Name – ask! and you will receive, that your joy might be full" [16:24]. Then St James comes along with "You ask and do not receive because you ask wrongly, in order to spend it on your pleasures" [4:3].

So, for what shall we pray? On the one hand, there is so much which is woven into suffering completely outside the punishment idea: there is cosmic significance, there is personal growth, there is the ability to touch others with a realistic help and comfort, there is simply the call to obedience, there is a relationship to the suffering of our Lord for the sake of the redemption of the universe, and more – do we dare cast aside such profound ramifications of suffering in order to cater to our luxury?

Yet on the other hand, suffering is, to put it mildly, very unpleasant. Do we not have the right to pray, "deliver us from evil [or the evil one?]" [Matthew 6:13]? Even Jesus asks "that, if possible, the hour might pass from Him … 'Abba, Father, all things are possible for You – remove this cup from Me; but, not what I desire, rather what You will'" [Mark 14:35-36] – however the puzzle here is that Jesus knows that there is no release from this destiny to which he has been born, so why this prayer? Is this just another example of a "useless" prayer?

Yes, it is wonderful to know that Jesus really does stand with us in not being excited about suffering. The down side is that it seems like the time when Henry Ford was asked if his Model T's could be of any other color. His reply was "Any customer can have a car painted any color he wants so long as it is black." Is it, as with Jesus also with us, that "Ask what you like, but you will have to go through this suffering anyway"? Why then should we request, and why should we intercede for others, if the suffering is necessary on a number of levels? Is it worthwhile praying at all?

At first glance, then, it seems that prayer is an exercise in futility – God will do what He chooses, although there is a vague carrot that perhaps something may actually happen in response to our requests. We are aware that Jehovah and we have different solutions to the problem of our suffering, as Yancey points out:

> I hesitate to write this, because it is a hard truth, and one I do not want to acknowledge. BUT JOB CONVINCES ME THAT GOD IS MORE INTERESTED IN OUR FAITH THAN IN OUR PLEASURE. Philip Yancey[77]

Returning to Jesus' prayer, it is not as if He is getting "cold feet," instead He simply spreads before His Father the turmoil which He is experiencing. He opens His heart to His Father, even when His yearnings are in conflict, that is, the God-given human instinct to preserve life struggles with the Spiritual purpose to redeem mankind. On the other hand, in His humility, He submits to the greater goal, not in resigned hopelessness but rather in a resurrection confidence, "for the joy set before Him." He makes no attempt at emotional or otherwise blackmail ("if You don't do this, then …") nor to

159

bargain through technique ("If I pray with more fervor, or if the format is just right, then …"). Instead, the nature of His prayer is a dialogue.

So also is Paul's prayer. Although strongly desiring to be rid of "the thorn," he not only expects his Lord to listen, *he* is willing to listen as well. Not feeling as though he is merely "stuck" with God's solution, rather he comes to understand that this suffering has an important usefulness, and now he can even rejoice in it. The attitude of dialogue is pivotal in prayer:

> My mother lived very close to God, and her example has influenced me greatly. When we asked her advice about anything, she would say, "I must ask God first." And we could not hurry her. Asking God was not a matter of spending five minutes to ask Him to bless her child and grant the request. It meant waiting upon God until she felt his leading. Whenever Mother prayed and trusted God for her decision, the undertaking invariably turned out well.   Madame Chiang Kai-Shek[78]

Such prayer is not a shopping list nor a "to-do" list nor even an ultimatum list, and too often we are not willing to allow God His timing in the process. Still it is set within an environment where God approaches us as His dearly beloved children and as His chosen co-workers in His universe – *a relationship of Love* in which He amazingly depends on us and we depend on Him. We ask (Matthew 18:19; Mark 11:24; Luke 11:9-13; John 14:13-14; 16:23-24), but always within the dialogue whose supreme objective is to become closer to each other and to His heart-felt purpose for humanity – and for us.

True, many things He cannot explain to us, and some decisions are based on a larger picture than we see, but ultimately "Fear not, little flock, for it is your Father's delight in giving you the Kingdom" [Luke 12:32]. So, yes, it is worthwhile to pray to our Father, Who is willing to "give good things to those who ask Him" [Matthew 7:11], but it is equally important to then listen very carefully for the rest of the dialogue.

Suffering's Ultimate Conclusion

One of the elders answered, saying to me, "These who are clothed with the white robes, who are they and from where did they come?" I said to him, "My lord, you know." He said to me, "These are they who have come out of the great tribulation; they have washed their robes and made them white in the Blood of the Lamb." Revelation 7:13-14

Previous to this passage are verses which describe the 144,000 from the tribes of Israel [vv 4-8], as well as the "great multitude which no man could number, of every nation, tribe, people and tongue … clothed with white robes" [v 9]. If indeed this is talking about all believers, as the description really leaves no other option (else there would needs be some other additional "great multitude"), then "the great tribulation" is living as God's people in this rebellion-tainted universe:

> 1. The low and desolate state they had formerly been in; they had been in great tribulation, persecuted by men, tempted by Satan, sometimes troubled in their own spirits; they had suffered the spoiling of their goods, the imprisonment of their persons, yea, the loss of life itself. The way to heaven lies through many tribulations; but tribulation, how great soever, shall not separate us from the love of God. …
> 2. The means by which they had been prepared for the great honour and happiness they now enjoyed: they had washed their robes, and made them white in the blood of the Lamb, Re 7:14. It is not the blood of the martyrs themselves, but the blood of the Lamb, that can wash away sin, and make the soul pure and clean in the sight of God. Other blood stains; this is the only blood that makes the robes of the saints white and clean. Matthew Henry[79]

However, it is not just that they stand before the Throne of God, but God's response in the following verses is:

> "They are before God's throne, and serve Him day and night in His temple. He Who sits on the throne will 'tent/camp' among them. They shall hunger no more nor thirst anymore; the sun shall not strike them, nor any heat; the Lamb Who is in the midst of the Throne will shepherd

them and lead them to Living Fountains of Waters, and God will wipe away every tear from their eyes." ...

I heard a great voice from heaven saying, "Behold, God's 'dwelling/tent' is with men, and He will 'dwell/camp' with them: they will be His People, God Himself will be with them and be their God. He will wipe away every tear from their eyes; death will be no more, nor grief, nor crying, nor pain any more, for the former things have passed away. He Who sits on the Throne says, "Behold, I make all things new." ...   Revelation 7:15-17; 21:3-5

This description is fascinating: not only will all "tribulation" be finished, but also, although our view of heaven is when "we get to dwell with God," *His* view of heaven is when He gets to dwell with us and to personally address the suffering which we have experienced. His desire to be with His People is depicted by the Tent of Meeting placed right in the middle of Israel in the wilderness; made visible by Jesus' birth in the midst of humanity; promised concerning His companionship whenever two or three are gathered in His Name; and on the Last Day it will be the attitude filled to overflowing by His eternal presence in the midst of His Blood-bought People.

But then, we also will be different:

Behold, I tell you a mystery: indeed not all of us will sleep, but we all will be transformed – in a moment, in the glance of an eye, at the Last Trumpet. For a trumpet will sound, and the dead will be raised imperishable, and we shall be changed. For it is absolutely necessary for this perishable to put on the imperishable; and this mortal to put on immortality. ... and as we have borne the image of the one made of dust, so also we will bear the image of the heavenly One.
                                                                I Corinthians 15:51-53, 49

How unimaginable it is to think we will be able to throw away this and every book on suffering! How wistfully we ponder Paul's statement that "the sufferings of this present time are not worthy in light of the Glory about to be revealed *in us*" [Roman 8:18]. No, suffering is not a

162

contradiction of life but rather the preparation for and the bold contrast of the eternal state which awaits us.

Joy

We end where we began, back to the Holy Innocents, whom the Church recognizes in the days after Christmas, who opens our door to the suffering of mankind ever since Adam and Eve stepped into rebellion. Just as the killing of the school children and adults in Newtown, mentioned above, occurred just before Christmas, these things fill us with indignation because they spoil the mood of the holiday. After all, the holiday is denoted by the angels tearing aside the curtain between heaven and earth as they fill the sky, celebrating the "good tidings of great joy which will be to all people" [Luke 2:10].

Yet these events do not intrude into the occasion, rather they are the explanation why this birth *had to happen*: Christmas is a most appropriate time for tragedies – it has everything to do with suffering, it was never meant to be a time of feeble sweetness nor of vague sentimental feelings. It is not meant to be comfortable! As the Child is born in that stable we already know what awaits Him: it is a Cross – there will be His own agony and death, His own abandonment from those He loves, and His own forsakenness from the One Who loves Him. This birth will pit the Creator against judgment, pain, death, and destruction; God Himself will personally stand victim of the cruelty and selfishness of sin's rebellion against Him, against what He is and against all for which He stands.

The message of the angels is not mere lighthearted gaiety nor meager empty well-wishing – there is a cost to the "peace and good will," but also a genuine joy which they declare. To their delight and astonishment, God has now started the process which will give life to all who would receive it. Here is a real power which prophesies the time when "the ransomed of Jehovah shall return ...with everlasting joy on their heads. They shall obtain joy and gladness, sorrow and sighing shall flee away" [Isaiah 51:11]. From the Baby in the manger to the King of the Jews hanging upon a Cross to the Resurrected Lord upon the Throne of the Universe, this strong joy holds its head above any dampening effect by the world's suffering.

In repentance, we realize that the path to the Cross, and what it has cost God Himself, is what *our* rebellion – *our* sin – has come to; but because God did not hesitate to bring Christmas into our world, we cannot escape the undercurrent of confidence and of rejoicing in that the Lord has the final say, and that we also will share in His victory. We can face whatever the world will throw at us with an answer which has grit and agony, and which conquers and gives eternal life.

We also know that this suffering does not merely randomly "happen," merely destroying without cause or purpose, but rather it is a far-reaching tool by which the Vinedresser nurtures greater fruit and greater goals, not just to a single person but to touch all in a tapestry which has great beauty and meaning in the end. We are not mere bystanders, nor are we merely patients of the Great Physician, but actual partners in His work before the universe, as was Job, Paul, Betsy, Corrie, Gordon, the prisoners in the death camps, those who have been "pruned," and those who have been "refined."

With each victory won because of suffering, won through suffering and won over suffering, we experience the harbinger of the final victory started on the Cross and to be completed on the Last Day, and we begin to understand the joy of which the angels sing. God the Son is wrapped in human Flesh and Blood, with all the pain receptors working both spiritually as well as physically. He has literally withheld nothing from us; He shares everything He is and has so that we now have that power, that of which angels declare, indeed a "great joy which shall be to all the people," not defeated or overwhelmed by tragedy or suffering, but rather that which stands on the solid rock of the Steadfast Love of God.

> At such times [of suffering] we focus too easily on our circumstances – our illnesses, our looks, our poverty, our bad luck – as the enemy. We pray for God to change our circumstances. If only I were beautiful or handsome, we think, then everything would work out . If only I had more money. Or at least a job. If only my sexual desires would somehow change, or at least diminish. Then I could easily believe God. But Job teaches that at the moment when faith is hardest and LEAST likely, then faith is most needed. Philip Yancey[80]

And, especially because of Jesus and the Holy Spirit, that faith is what we have.

Endnotes

1 Clive Staples Lewis, *The Problem of Pain*, 59

2 Tom Long, "Preaching About Suffering" (Grant R. Macdonald, St. Andrew s Presb, Kitchener; Internet: (87/10/26))

3 Clive Staples Lewis, *The Great Divorce*

4 James Lindemann, *In the Image of God: Male and Female He Created Them*, 1-2

5 Ibid, 42

6 Lewis, *Pain*, 66

7 I Thessalonians 4:15-17:

> For this we say to you in the Word of the Lord, that we the living who remain until the coming of the Lord will by no means precede those who have fallen asleep. For the Lord Himself – in a shout, in the sound of the archangel, and in a trumpet of God – will descend from heaven. The dead in Christ will rise first, then we who are alive and are left, together with them, will be taken up in clouds to meet the Lord in the air and thus always we will be with the Lord.

8 The Hebrew root also denotes "freedom"; but consider Jeremiah 34, "Because of their hypocrisy, the prophet announced that the people would be 'set free' – to the sword, pestilence, and famine (vv. 15-17)" [TWOT #454b]

9 Paul Brand and Philip Yancey, *The Gift of Pain*, Zondervan Publishing House, Grand Rapids, Michigan. 1997. Previously titled "Pain: The Gift Nobody Wants"

10 Philip Yancey, "Pain: the Tool of the Wounded Surgeon," *Christianity Today* (March 24, 1978), 14.

11 Paul Brand, "Why One Doctor Prays for Pain," *Eternity Magazine* (October, 1975), 20.

12 Brand, *The Gift*, 187-188.

13 Brand, "Doctor Prays," 19.

14 Christopher Townsend, "Hell: a difficult doctrine we dare not ignore," Cambridge Papers: Vol 8 No 3 (September 1999); http://www.jubilee-centre.org/document.php?id=25; retrieved 2013-05-01.

15 Luther, "In Conclusion," *Large Catechism*.

16 Townsend, "Hell."

17 Lewis, *Divorce*, 75.

18 Yancey, "the Tool," 15.

19 Corrie ten Boom, *The Hiding Place* (Fleming H Revell Company: Old Tappen, New Jersey, 1971), 198-199.

20 Ibid, 195.

21 Ibid, 238.

22 Ibid, 175.

23 Ibid, 180.

24 Ibid, 194-195

25 Actually the Hebrew text reads, "Bless God and die," but the tone is sarcastic.

26 Philip Yancey, "When The Facts Don't Add Up," Christian Bible Studies, 7/09/2008, http://www.christianitytoday.com/biblestudies/articles/theology/080709 .html, retrieved 2013-05-28.

27 "seven sons and three daughters" [Job 1:2] – "seven" is the only Hebrew number that is also a word, the word for the "oath" used in Covenant.. Often there seems to be a subliminal messaging in many circumstances where this number appears, an emphasis that the events have something to do with a person or nation's connection to Jehovah, for example, when Israel takes Jericho [Joshua 6:1-20]. As well, "three" and "ten" are not merely random numbers.

28 Yancey, "When The Facts"

29 This word means "a setting forth, the show-bread; predetermination, purpose" – what is set before all in regard to God's plan.

30 From the author's presentation on the backgrounds of common hymns.

31 Ibid.

32 Ernest Gordon, *Through the Valley of the Kwai* (Harper & Brothers: New York, 1962)

33 Ibid, 58-59.

34 Ibid, 77-78.

35 Clive Staples Lewis, *A Grief Observed*, Harper Collins Publishers: New York, reprint 1989, 18.

36 James Lindemann, *Creation's Ballet for Jesus*, RFLindemann & Son, 2011

37 Ibid, 153.

38 Ibid, 137.

39 Ibid, 139-140.

40 Ibid, 204.

41 The Holy Spirit appears to be already active "in the world": there is not only Job as Abraham's contemporary but also Melchizedek, "Priest of the Most High God" [Genesis 14:28], "to whom even the patriarch Abraham gave a tenth of the spoils" [Hebrews 7:4].

42 John emphasizes that faith and "overcoming the world" occur in the context of a close, personal relationship with God. The depth of that relationship has become far more "visible" in the New Testament, and "born of God" is a powerful way to describe it. Yet there is a close personal counterpart which we see with Abraham and other Old Testament saints: although they may not have the awareness of all the details that the Christian now understands, they have Covenant with God.

The joining in Covenant is most powerful: it is an intermingling of Life (Soul) and Love [I Samuel 18:1,3]. It revolves around the mutual blending of Blood between its participants, which, according to Genesis 9:4 and Deuteronomy 12:23, is also the blending of "Life" and "Soul" [see this author's book *Covenant: The Blood is The Life*]. In that context, Covenant with Jehovah is to have His Life, His "Soul," coursing through one's "veins."

Looking at the scene in heaven in Revelation, although there appears to be a separate status for the Israelite (the "144,000" [7:4-8]), there appears to be no division among "the great multitude which no one could number" [v 9] – it seems there will be no distinction between Noah, Job, Melchizedek and New Testament believers like you and me: all are "born of God," all are in Covenant. Again, the Old Testament believer will experience the fullness of Jesus' and the Holy Spirit's gifts without distinction because the benefits of Jesus and Pentecost flow backward as well as forward.

[43] Ibid, 188:

The Railroad of Death had long since been finished. The originally estimated five- to six-year project that was to have been completed in eighteen months had taken only twelve. But the toll in suffering endured and lives lost was fantastic. The railroad was two hundred and fifty miles long. Every mile of it cost, on an average, the lives of sixty-four [16,000 – about 1 every 27 yards/meters] prisoners of war and two hundred and forty [60,000 – about 1 every 7 yards/meters] Southeast Asians.

For every football field size length, there will be 18 bodies, along with how many amputations from sickness and/or injury, although there would be a higher cluster of deaths around the bridge itself. This makes the story, *The Bridge Over the River Kwai*, although a study in the British sense of pride, a seeming trivializing of the suffering and death of the real prisoners, much less a diversion from the real Savior of those in the camps, which is not pride, but Jesus.

[44] Ibid, 146.

[45] Yancey, "The Facts"

[46] ten Boom, 194-195

[47] Gordon, 139-140

[48] Oral Roberts, "How To Recover It All," *Charisma & Christian Life* Magazine (September 1988).

[49] Charles Spurgeon, *The Power of Prayer in a Believer's Life*, Ed by Robert Hall (Emerald Books, 1993), p 81-81

[50] Lawrence Mbogoni, http://www.h-net.org/~africa/threads/village.html, retrieved 2013-07-18. Although the discussion about the "proverb" could not identify its source, it identified that many cultures in both Africa and North America practiced the concept. In a later post he writes:

While it is interesting to seek provenance in regard to the proverb, "It takes a village to raise a child," I think it would be misleading to ascribe its origin to a single source. As I noted in my earlier message, some of us do relate to it as part of our backgrounds. Let me give a few examples of African societies with proverbs which translate to "It takes a village...":

In Lunyoro (Banyoro) there is a proverb that says "Omwana talwalila nju emoi," whose literal translation is A child does not grow up only in a single home."

In Kihaya (Bahaya) there is a saying, "Omwana taba womoi," which translates as "A child belongs not to one parent or home."

In Kijita (Wajita) there is a proverb which says "Omwana ni wa bhone," meaning regardless of a child's biological parent(s) its upbringing belongs to the community.

In Kiswahili the proverb "Asiyefunzwa na mamae hufunzwa na ulimwengu" approximates to the same.

51 Claire Dehon, Ibid.

52 George S. Steward, *The Lower Levels of Prayer* (Cokesbury Press, 1940), 107

53 http://www.pnas.org/misc/archive033103.shtml

54 http://www.orgonomy.org/article_027.html; also http://www.pathlights.com /Public%20Enemies/dope_on_drugs2.htm

55 James Lindemann, "Discipleship Course" Bible study.

56 Ibid.

57 Roger Lancelyn Green & Walter Hooper; C.S. Lewis: A Biography (New York: Harcourt Brace Jovanovich, 1974), 105

58 Lewis, *Divorce*

59 *Exodus*, in *The Pulpit Commentary*, ed. H.D.M. Spence and Joseph S. Exell, (NY, NY: Funk & Wagnalls Company, 1950), 291:

> Imperfection attaches to everything that man does; and even the sacrifices that the people offered to God required to be atoned for and purified. It was granted to the high priest in his official capacity to make the necessary atonement, and so render the people's gifts acceptable.

Concordia Self-Study Commentary, ed., Walter R. Roehrs and Martin H Franzmann, (St Louis: Concordia Publishing House, 1979), 82:

> *Holy to the Lord.* This inscription epitomized the significance of his office. God, as it were, laid His hand on his forehead as if to declare him a sacrificial offering to the Lord (cf. 29:10; Lv 4:4). Furthermore *any guilt* incurred in the holy offering ... rested on his head. But functioning as a divinely appointed mediator, he nevertheless bore before his eyes the constant assurance that through his mediation the people's offering was *accepted before the Lord.* The High Priest who actualized what Aaron's tiara symbolized wore as His headdress a crown of thorns. (Mt 27:29)

60 James Lindemann, *Covenant: The Blood is The Life* (RFLindemann & Son, 2011), 159

61 Pashhur struck Jeremiah the prophet, and put him in the stocks that were in the upper Benjamin Gate of the house of Jehovah [Jeremiah 20:2]

The princes, enraged at Jeremiah, beat him and put him into prison in the house of Jonathan the scribe for they had made the house a prison. When Jeremiah had come into the dungeon and into the cell, he stayed there many days. [Jeremiah 37:15-16]

They took Jeremiah and cast him into the cistern of Malchiah son of Melech, which was in the court of the prison, letting Jeremiah down by ropes – there was no water in the cistern, but only mud, and Jeremiah sank in the mud. [Jeremiah 38:6]

[62] I say, "I will not make mention Him, nor speak anymore in His Name" – but in my heart it becomes like a burning fire shut up in my bones; I am weary of holding it in, and I cannot. [Jeremiah 20:9]

[63] Woe is me, my mother, that you bore me, a man of strife, a man of contention, to all the land! I am neither lender nor borrower, yet all curse me. … I will make you to this people a fortified wall of bronze; although they fight against you, they will not prevail over you, for I am with you to save you and to deliver you, declares Jehovah. [Jeremiah 15:10, 20]

Then they said, "Come, let us devise plans against Jeremiah, for the law will not perish from the priest, nor counsel from the wise, nor the word from the prophet. Come, let us pummel him with the tongue and not give heed any of his words" [Jeremiah 18:18]

[64] I did not sit in the council of mockers, nor was I haughty; because Your hand was upon me I sat alone, for You filled me with indignation. Why has my pain been unceasing, my wound incurable, refusing to be healed? Are You not like a deceptive mirage to me, like waters that fail? [Jeremiah 15:17-18]

You deceived me, O Jehovah, and I was deceived; You are stronger than I and have prevailed. I am a laughingstock all the day; every one mocks me. For whenever I speak, I cry out, I proclaim, "Violence and devastation!" For the Word of Jehovah has been to me a reproach and derision all day long. [Jeremiah 20:7-8]

Cursed is the day on which I was born! The day in which my mother bore me, let it not be blessed! Cursed is the man who brought news to my father, "A son is born to you," making him very glad. … Why did I come forth from the womb to see toil and sorrow, and spend my days in shame? [Jeremiah 20:14-18]

[65] I was like like a gentle lamb led to the slaughter; I did not know it was against me they devised plans, saying, "Destroy the tree with its fruit; cut him off from the land of the living, make his name remembered no more!" But Jehovah of hosts judges righteously and tries the innermost being and the heart – let me see Your vengeance upon them, for to You have I committed my cause. [Jeremiah 11:19-20]

Jehovah, You know all their counsel against me, to kill me. Do not atone [KAPHAR] their iniquity, nor blot out their sin from Your sight; but let them stagger before You: deal with them in the time of Your anger. [Jeremiah 18:23]

[66] The word in the Greek is difficult to express: it can be translated as "glorious" (KJV and NKJV), or "dignitaries" (RSV), but the thrust of his argument does not seem to be talking about humans, but rather about satanic beings; therefore "dazzling" is chosen so as to reflect II Corinthians 11:14-15:

no wonder! For Satan masquerades himself as an angel of light. Therefore it is no great thing if his servants also masquerade as servants of righteousness, whose end will be according to their works

[67] James Lindemann, *Spiritual Warfare*, soon to be published.

68 The song, "Devil went down to Georgia" (Charlie Daniels Band) and the short story "The Devil and Daniel Webster" (Stephen Vincent Benét), among others.

69 Lindemann, *Warfare*

70 Ibid.

71 Yancey, "The Facts"

72 Robert F Lindemann, from an unpublished Trinity Sunday sermon.

73 In 1850 a teenager who was deeply troubled about how he might be saved found it impossible to go to his usual church. It had snowed so much that he was forced to turn aside, ultimately to end up in a little chapel. At first, no minister showed up.

At last a very thin looking man came into the pulpit and opened his Bible and read these words: 'Look unto Me, and be ye saved all the ends of the earth.'

Just setting his eyes upon me, as if he knew me all by heart, he said: 'Young man, you are in trouble.' Well, I was, sure enough. Says he, 'You will never get out of it unless you look to Christ.'

And then, lifting up his hands, he cried out, ... 'Look, look, look. – it's only look!' said he. I saw at once the way of salvation. Oh, how I did leap for joy at that moment! I know not what else he said: I did not take much notice of it -- I was so possessed with that one thought. Like as when the brazen serpent was lifted up, they only looked and were healed. I had been waiting to do fifty things, but when I heard this word, 'Look!' what a charming word it seemed to me. Oh, I looked until I could almost have looked my eyes away."

The teenager? Charles Spurgeon! ... See in God's providential ordering of things which led to Spurgeon's salvation: the snowstorm, the change in Spurgeon's plans, the absence of the usual minister, the presence of the thin looking man, his choice of text and his bold confrontation of the teenager – all contributed to Spurgeon's conversion.

Unknown

74 Yancey, "The Facts"

75 Ibid.

76 Ibid.

77 Yancey, "The Facts"

78 Madame Chiang Kai-Shek, in "The United States News," as quoted in *The Speakers Book of Illustrative Stories* (Maxwell Droke: Droke House, Indianapolis, 1956), 265

79 Matthew Henry, *Matthew Henry Commentary*, Unabridged Edition, based on the Fleming H. Revell Edition, added for electronic use with the "Online Bible" (version 2.99), Timnathserah Inc. (Winterbourne, Ontario: 1997; http://www.onlinebible.net)); commentary on Revelation 7:14.

80 Yancey, "The Facts"